EGYPT TRAVEL

Guide to the Land of Mystique, with the essential Tips to Explore the Great Egyptian Wonders, Pyramids, Mummies and Ancient Cities.

All rights reserved. No part of this publication may be reproduced, distributed, or transmitted in any form or by any means, including photocopying, recording, or other electronic or mechanical methods, without the express written permission of the publisher

except for the use of brief quotations in a book review.

Copyright © Terry M. Zavala, 2023.

Table of Contents

Chapter one

Introduction

- Overview of Egypt
- Brief History of Egypt
- Culture, geography and Climate Nature in Egypt

Chapter Two

Getting ready for your Trip to Egypt

- Before your Trip
- Entry requirements
- Visa requirements (where to get your Visa)
- Best time to visit Egypt

- Rules guiding Visitors in Egypt
- Budget Tips for your Trip
- Currency
- Safety precautions

Chapter Three

Vital tips for your trip

- Moving around Egypt (Transportation: Taxi, Train, Feluccas)
- Accommodation: Hotels and Hostels
- Language: Arabic Phrases for Travelers
- Egypt Cultural Value
- Ethics of Life
- Egypt's local dishes

- Egypt's Local Drinks
- Shopping in Egypt

  *Cairo Market

  * Khan Market

  * Luxor Market

  * Aswan Market

Chapter Four

Tourism in Egypt / places to Visit

- Cairo: The Capital of Egypt
- Alexandria
- Siwa Oasis
- Aswan
- Luxor

- Fayoum
- Edfu
- Nile and the City of the dead

<u>Chapter Five</u>

Customs in Egypt

- Egyptian Religion: Mosques, Synagogues, Coptic Churches
- Egyptian museum
- Arts and Crafts in Egypt
- Dressing Culture in Egypt
- Music and Dance
- Nightlife in Egypt

Chapter Six

Activities to engage on in Egypt

- Snorkeling
- Camel Riding
- Hiking
- Hot Air Ballooning

Chapter Seven

Egyptian Wonders

- Egyptian mummies
- The Sphinx
- Karnak Temple
- The pyramids of Giza

Final Tips for your stay and visit in Egypt

Before leaving Egypt

Egyptian souvenirs to take home

Goodbye from Egypt

Chapter one

INTRODUCTION

Overview of Egypt

Egypt, often referred to as the "Gift of the Nile," is a captivating country that exudes a sense of timelessness and wonder. Nestled in the northeastern corner of Africa, it stands as a bridge between the African and Asian continents, with its rich history and remarkable geography making it one of the world's most enticing destinations.

At the heart of Egypt's allure lies its ancient heritage. This land was once home to one of the world's most advanced civilizations, the mighty Egyptians, whose ingenuity gave rise to the awe-inspiring pyramids, colossal temples, and elaborate tombs that continue to astound visitors today. The iconic Pyramids of Giza, including the Great Pyramid of Khufu, remain enduring symbols of human achievement.

The Nile River, the lifeblood of Egypt, weaves through the country like a silver ribbon, nurturing the fertile Nile Delta and sustaining an unbroken agricultural tradition dating back millennia. Beyond its historical significance, the river is also a source of recreation, with Nile cruises offering travelers a unique perspective of Egypt's landscapes and culture.

Egypt's cities are a blend of the ancient and the modern. Cairo, the sprawling capital, pulses with energy, housing both historic wonders like the Egyptian Museum and bustling markets, as well as contemporary marvels like skyscrapers and vibrant nightlife. Luxor and Aswan provide glimpses into Egypt's past, with temples and tombs that harken back to the glory days of the Pharaohs.

The Red Sea coastline draws sun-seekers and water enthusiasts to its pristine shores, offering opportunities for diving, snorkeling, and relaxation in world-renowned resorts like Sharm El Sheikh and Hurghada.

Egypt's culinary scene is a feast of flavors, with aromatic spices and fresh ingredients crafting dishes like koshari, falafel, and shawarma that tantalize the taste buds. Hospitality is ingrained in Egyptian culture, and visitors can expect warm welcomes and genuine interactions.

As you embark on your journey through Egypt, prepare to be immersed in a world where history, culture, and natural beauty converge to create an unforgettable experience. Egypt, with its ancient treasures and warm hospitality, beckons travelers to uncover its timeless mysteries and modern delights.

History of Egypt

The history of Egypt spans over five millennia, making it one of the world's oldest civilizations. Its storied past unfolds like chapters in a timeless epic, with each era leaving an indelible mark on the nation's identity.

Ancient Egypt (c. 3100 BC - 332 BC): The history of Egypt begins with the unification of Upper and Lower Egypt around 3100 BC, under the rule of King Menes. This marked the birth of the first Pharaonic dynasty. Ancient Egypt flourished as a powerful empire, characterized by the construction of colossal pyramids, intricate hieroglyphics, and a pantheon of gods. Notable pharaohs include Khufu, Ramses II, and Tutankhamun. The civilization's achievements in medicine, mathematics, and architecture were unparalleled in their time.

Ptolemaic and Roman Period (332 BC - 395 AD): In 332 BC, Alexander the Great conquered Egypt, initiating the Ptolemaic era. Cleopatra, the last Pharaoh of Egypt, is a legendary figure from this time. Egypt then became a province of the Roman Empire in 30 BC, blending Egyptian and Greco-Roman cultures.

Byzantine and Islamic Egypt (395 AD - 641 AD): With the fall of the Roman Empire, Egypt came under Byzantine rule until the Arab-Muslim conquest in 641 AD. The introduction of Islam brought profound changes, including the Arabic language and Islamic architecture. The founding of Cairo in 969 AD as Egypt's new capital marked a pivotal moment.

Medieval and Ottoman Egypt (1517 AD - 1805 AD): Egypt became part of the Ottoman Empire in 1517, with Cairo as a regional center. The French briefly occupied Egypt in the late 18th century, leading to the rise of Muhammad Ali Pasha, who modernized the country and established a dynasty.

Modern Egypt (1805 AD - Present): Egypt's modern history is marked by colonialism, nationalism, and political upheaval. In 1922,

Egypt gained partial independence from Britain. Full independence came in 1952, following a revolution led by Gamal Abdel Nasser.

Egypt remains a prominent player in the Arab world and the Middle East. Its rich history is a source of national pride, with ancient monuments, such as the Pyramids and the Sphinx, standing as enduring symbols of the country's legacy. Today, Egypt is a vibrant, culturally diverse nation that continues to evolve, honoring its past while embracing the challenges and opportunities of the present and the future

Culture, geography and Climate Nature in Egypt

Egypt is not only renowned for its ancient wonders but also for its rich cultural heritage, diverse geography, and unique climate. This triad of culture, geography, and climate shapes the natural aspects of the country.

Culture:

Egypt's culture has been influenced by a myriad of civilizations, from the Pharaonic era to Greek, Roman, Arab, and Ottoman rule. Today, Egypt's cultural identity is a fusion of ancient customs and contemporary expressions.

Egyptian culture is a fascinating blend of ancient heritage and contemporary influences, shaped by millennia of history. It stands as a testament to the enduring legacy of this ancient civilization.

The majority of Egyptians are Muslim, with a significant Coptic Christian minority. Islamic traditions play a vital role in daily life, including religious holidays and festivals.

Egypt's rich cultural heritage also, is most notably expressed through its historical treasures. The majestic pyramids, intricate hieroglyphics, and grand temples showcase the artistic and architectural prowess of ancient Egyptians.

Moreover, amalgamation of cultures has left a lasting imprint on Egyptian art, cuisine, and customs.

Egyptian culture offers travelers a unique opportunity to immerse themselves in a world where ancient traditions coexist with modern influences. Whether exploring historical sites, savoring local cuisine, or experiencing the warmth of Egyptian hospitality, this culture is an integral part of the country's allure.

Geography:

Egypt's geography is of diverse landscapes, with the Nile River as its defining feature.

The Nile River: This life-giving river winds through the country from south to north, creating a narrow fertile strip known as the Nile Delta. It sustains agriculture, enabling Egypt to flourish in an otherwise arid landscape.

Desert Regions: The vast Sahara Desert dominates the rest of Egypt's territory. The Western Desert, with its rolling dunes and oases, offers desert adventures and historical sites like the Siwa Oasis. The Eastern Desert is home to mountains and the Red Sea coast.

Climate:

Egypt's climate is characterized by its arid nature, with three distinct seasons.

Summer (June-August): Summers are sweltering, especially in the south. Temperatures in Luxor and Aswan can exceed 100°F (37°C). Coastal areas provide some relief, with sea breezes moderating the heat.

Winter (December-February): Winters are milder and more comfortable for travelers, with temperatures ranging from 50°F (10°C) in Cairo to 70°F (21°C) in Aswan. This is the peak tourist season.

Spring and Autumn: These transitional seasons offer pleasant weather and are ideal for exploring Egypt's historical sites without the extremes of summer or winter.

Despite its arid climate, Egypt boasts unique natural beauty.

In Egypt, culture, geography, and climate converge to create a multifaceted natural experience. From the historical treasures along the Nile to the awe-inspiring desert landscapes and the vibrant culture that infuses daily life, Egypt is a destination that offers a rich carpet of experiences for travelers.

Chapter Two

Getting ready for your Trip to Egypt

Before your Trip

Embarking on a journey to Egypt, a country teeming with millennia of history and cultural treasures, is a thrilling prospect. However, to ensure a smooth and enriching experience, meticulous preparations are key. Here's a comprehensive guide to getting ready for your trip to Egypt:

1. Passport and Visa:

Check your passport's expiration date, ensuring it's valid for at least six months beyond your planned departure date.

Research Egypt's visa requirements based on your nationality. Many travelers can obtain a visa on arrival, while others may need to apply in advance through an Egyptian embassy or online.

2. Health Preparations:

Consult with your healthcare provider to review recommended vaccinations and health precautions for Egypt. Ensure you have necessary prescriptions and medications.

Consider purchasing travel insurance that covers medical emergencies, trip cancellations, and lost luggage.

3. Research and Itinerary:

Study Egypt's geography, regions, and attractions to create an itinerary tailored to your interests. Prioritize must-visit historical sites, cultural experiences, and natural wonders.

Plan a flexible itinerary that allows for spontaneous discoveries and relaxation.

4. Packing Essentials:

Pack clothing suitable for the climate. Lightweight, breathable fabrics are essential, especially in the desert regions.

Don't forget essentials like sunscreen, sunglasses, a wide-brimmed hat, comfortable walking shoes, and a swimsuit if you plan to visit coastal areas.

5. Currency and Payments:

Exchange some currency for Egyptian Pounds (EGP) before your trip for initial expenses, but be prepared to withdraw cash from ATMs in Egypt.

Notify your bank about your travel plans to avoid card issues and withdrawal restrictions.

Familiarize yourself with basic Arabic phrases to facilitate communication with locals. English is commonly spoken in tourist areas.

Consider purchasing a local SIM card or an international roaming plan for your phone to access maps and stay connected.

6. Electrical Adapters:

Egypt uses Type C and Type F electrical outlets. Bring appropriate travel adapters and voltage converters if your devices require them.

7. Travel Documents and Copies:

Keep printed and digital copies of important travel documents, including your passport, visa, itinerary, and insurance details. Store them securely and separately from the originals.

8. Travel Insurance:

- Consider purchasing comprehensive travel insurance covering medical emergencies, trip cancellations, and theft. Ensure you understand the coverage details and carry a copy of your policy.

Book your accommodation well in advance, especially if you're traveling during peak tourist seasons. Consider airport transfers or research local transportation options.

9. Travel Vaccinations:

Visit a travel clinic or healthcare provider for recommended vaccinations and health advice specific to Egypt. Ensure you have essential medications and a basic first-aid kit.

Getting ready for your trip to Egypt involves thoughtful planning and preparations that will set the stage for an unforgettable adventure. With these comprehensive steps in mind, you'll be well-prepared to explore Egypt's iconic historical sites, immerse yourself in its rich culture, and create lasting memories.

Entry requirements

Visa requirements **(where to** get your Visa)

Egypt, a land of ancient wonders and cultural treasures, welcomes travelers from around the world. To ensure a smooth entry into the country, it's crucial to understand the visa requirements and where to obtain your visa. Here's a comprehensive guide for travelers:

1. **Visa Requirements by Nationality:**

Egypt has varying visa requirements depending on your nationality. Most travelers can obtain a visa on arrival (VOA) at major Egyptian airports and land border crossings.

VOA typically allows for a stay of up to 30 days and can be extended for an additional 30 days while in Egypt.

2. Countries Exempt from Visa Requirements:

Some nationalities are exempt from obtaining a visa for Egypt. These countries include most Arab and Middle Eastern nations, as well as some African and Asian countries.

Check the official website of the Egyptian Ministry of Foreign Affairs for an updated list of exempted countries.

3. Visa Extensions: If you wish to extend your stay beyond the initial 30 days granted by the VOA, you can do so at the Passport, Immigration, and Nationality Administration office in Egypt.

It's recommended to initiate the extension process at least a week before your original visa's expiration date.

4. Visa Types:

Tourist Visa: This is the most common visa type for travelers. It allows for sightseeing, exploring historical sites, and enjoying Egypt's attractions.

Business Visa: If you intend to engage in business activities or attend conferences, a business visa is required. You should apply for this visa in advance through the Egyptian embassy or consulate in your home country.

Work Visa: Individuals planning to work in Egypt need a work visa, which should be arranged by their employer in Egypt prior to their arrival.

Student Visa: Students planning to study in Egypt must apply for a student visa through the Egyptian embassy or consulate.

5. Obtaining a Visa in Advance: While VOA is convenient for many travelers, some nationalities are required to obtain their visas in advance through an Egyptian embassy or consulate in their home country.

To apply for a visa in advance, you will typically need to provide a completed application form, a valid passport, a passport-sized photo, proof of accommodation, and a copy of your flight itinerary.

6. Visa Fees:

Visa fees vary depending on the type of visa and your nationality. Check the website of the Egyptian embassy or consulate in your country for current visa fees and payment methods.

Visa validity periods can vary based on the type of visa and your nationality. Ensure that your visa will cover the duration of your stay in Egypt and any planned extensions.

7. Visa on Arrival Process:

Upon arrival at an Egyptian airport or land border crossing, proceed to the Visa on Arrival desk.

Complete the visa application form provided at the desk.

Pay the visa fee in cash (typically in US dollars or Euros). It's advisable to have the exact amount as change may not be readily available.

Receive your visa sticker and affix it to your passport.

9. Entry and Exit Stamps:

Ensure that your passport is stamped both upon entry and exit from Egypt. Failure to do so may result in fines or delays when leaving the country.

Before your trip to Egypt, it's essential to check the most up-to-date visa requirements and procedures based on your nationality. By understanding Egypt's entry requirements, you can start your journey with confidence and enjoy the rich history and culture this incredible country has to offer.

Best time to visit Egypt

Egypt, with its iconic historical sites, mesmerizing landscapes, and rich culture, is a year-round destination. However, the best time to visit depends on your preferences and the experiences you seek. Here's a guide to help you choose the ideal time for your Egyptian adventure:

High Season (October to April):

October to November and February to April: These months are considered the peak tourist season in Egypt due to the pleasant weather. Temperatures are mild, making it comfortable for exploring historical sites, such as the Pyramids of Giza, Luxor, and Abu Simbel.

December to January: This is the coolest time of the year in Egypt, making it ideal for those who prefer milder temperatures. It's especially great for exploring outdoor attractions like the temples of Karnak and the Valley of the Kings.

Shoulder Season (May to September): May to June: As spring transitions into early summer, temperatures start to rise. This period is ideal for travelers who want to avoid crowds and can handle warmer weather.

July to August: Egypt experiences its hottest months during July and August, with temperatures often exceeding 100°F (38°C) in many areas. While the heat can be intense, it's an excellent time for diving and snorkeling in the Red Sea coastal resorts of Sharm El Sheikh and Hurghada.

September: By late September, temperatures begin to cool down slightly, making it a good time for exploring cultural and historical sites. However, it can still be hot in southern Egypt, so be prepared for warm weather.

Considerations:

Ramadan: Ramadan, the Islamic holy month of fasting, has a significant impact on travel in Egypt. It follows the Islamic lunar calendar, so its timing shifts each year. During Ramadan, many restaurants and cafes may be closed during the day, and public transportation schedules may be adjusted. However, it can be a unique cultural experience to witness local traditions and nighttime celebrations.

Special Events:

If you're interested in experiencing Egyptian festivals and cultural events, consider planning your trip around:

Eid al-Fitr: This festive holiday marks the end of Ramadan and is celebrated with feasts and gatherings.

Abu Simbel Sun Festival: Twice a year, on February 22 and October 22, the sunlight aligns with the statues in the Abu Simbel temples, creating a spectacular visual phenomenon.

Coptic Christmas: Celebrated on January 7, Coptic Christmas is an important religious holiday in Egypt, marked by church services and celebrations.

Ultimately, the best time to visit Egypt depends on your travel preferences. If you prefer milder weather and fewer crowds, consider the shoulder seasons. For a comfortable exploration of historical sites, the high season is ideal. If you're a diving enthusiast, the summer months provide excellent underwater visibility in the Red Sea. Regardless of when you visit, Egypt promises a wealth of historical, cultural, and natural wonders waiting to be explored.

Rules guiding Visitors in Egypt

Visiting Egypt, a country steeped in history and rich in cultural traditions, is an exciting and enriching experience. To ensure a respectful and enjoyable journey for yourself and the local community, it's essential to be aware of and adhere to certain rules and guidelines:

Respect for Religious Sites:

When visiting mosques, churches, and temples, dress modestly. Both men and women should cover their shoulders, knees, and cleavage. Remove your shoes before entering religious buildings.

Avoid visiting during prayer times, and always follow the guidance of local staff and religious leaders.

Photography and Video Recording:

Always ask for permission before taking photos of individuals, especially women. Some people may decline, so respect their wishes.

In certain areas, like archaeological sites and museums, photography may be restricted or require a special permit. Respect these rules.

Public Displays of Affection: Egypt is a conservative country, so it's best to refrain from public displays of affection. Holding hands is generally acceptable for couples, but more intimate gestures should be reserved for private settings.

Local Customs and Etiquette:

Greet people with a polite "Salaam alaykum" (peace be upon you) or "Hello." It's customary to respond with "Wa alaykum salaam" (and peace be upon you).

It's polite to remove your shoes when entering someone's home, and it's customary to bring a small gift, like sweets or fruit, when visiting.

Be respectful of local customs, such as the practice of bargaining in markets, and engage in friendly negotiation with vendors.

Alcohol is available in Egypt but may not be as prevalent or easily accessible as in some Western countries. Respect local regulations and customs regarding alcohol consumption.

Tipping, locally known as "baksheesh," is customary and appreciated by service workers. Be prepared to tip tour guides, drivers, hotel staff, and restaurant servers based on the level of service.

It's customary to tip restroom attendants in public facilities.

If your visit coincides with Ramadan, be respectful of fasting hours and avoid eating, drinking, or smoking in public during daylight hours. Many restaurants and cafes will be closed during the day, but will open for evening meals.

Be respectful of local customs and traditions, and try to engage with the local community in a culturally sensitive and responsible manner.

By keeping to these you will have a more enjoyable experience and authentic experience in Egypt.

Budget Tips for your Trip

Traveling to Egypt, with its stunning landmarks, can be a budget-friendly adventure if you plan wisely. Here are some budget tips to help you make the most of your trip without breaking the bank:

Off-Peak Travel:

In your budget, consider visiting during the shoulder or low seasons, typically during the summer months. Prices for accommodation and tours may be lower, and you can avoid the crowds at popular attractions.

Accommodation Choices:

Opt for budget-friendly accommodation options, such as guesthouses, hostels, and budget hotels.

Many offer comfortable amenities at a fraction of the cost of luxury hotels.

Consider booking accommodation with included breakfast to save on dining expenses.

Local Cuisine:

Explore Egypt's diverse and affordable street food. Dishes like koshari, falafel, and ta'ameya (Egyptian falafel) are not only delicious but also budget-friendly.

Eat at local restaurants and cafeterias, where you can enjoy authentic Egyptian meals at lower prices compared to tourist-oriented establishments.

Transportation:

Use public transportation, such as buses and local taxis, to get around cities and towns. They are cost-effective and offer a glimpse into local life.

If you're traveling with a group, consider renting a car and splitting the costs, which can be economical, especially when visiting multiple destinations.

Guided Tours:

Instead of expensive private tours, join group tours for visits to historical sites. Group tours are often more affordable and provide valuable insights from knowledgeable guides.

Research free or low-cost guided tours offered by some hostels and hotels.

Entrance Fees and Passes:

Invest in a multi-site pass, like the Luxor Pass or Cairo Pass, if you plan to visit multiple historical sites. These passes can offer significant savings on entrance fees.

Keep your student ID handy if you have one, as it may grant you discounts at museums and historical sites.

Water and Hydration:

Drink bottled water to stay hydrated, but be mindful of your water consumption to avoid excessive costs. Consider carrying a reusable water bottle and refilling it from safe sources when possible.

ATMs and Currency Exchange:

Use ATMs to withdraw Egyptian Pounds (EGP) for your expenses. ATMs are widely available in cities and tourist areas, and they offer competitive exchange rates.

Exchange a small amount of currency before your trip to cover initial expenses, but be cautious of unfavorable rates at airports.

Free and Low-Cost Activities:

Enjoy the many free and low-cost activities in Egypt, like wandering through local markets, taking leisurely strolls along the Nile Corniche, and exploring charming neighborhoods.

Currency

Understanding the currency and monetary system in Egypt is essential for a smooth and enjoyable travel experience. Here's a guide to Egypt's currency, banking, and money-related tips for travelers:

Currency: The official currency of Egypt is the Egyptian Pound, denoted by the symbol "EGP" and often abbreviated as "LE" (short for "livre égyptienne" in French). The Egyptian Pound is further divided into smaller units called "piastres," with 100 piastres equaling 1 Egyptian Pound. While piastres are still used in daily transactions, prices are often quoted in pounds.

Banknotes and Coins: Egyptian banknotes come in various denominations, including 1, 5, 10, 20, 50, 100, and 200 pounds. Coins are less commonly used but come in 1, 5, 10, 25, and 50 piastre denominations. It's essential to have a mix of notes and coins for small purchases, as some vendors may prefer cash over cards for minor transactions.

Foreign Currency: While the Egyptian Pound is the official currency, some businesses and hotels in major tourist areas, particularly in Cairo and Luxor, may accept US dollars and euros. However, it's always recommended to use

Egyptian Pounds for transactions to avoid unfavorable exchange rates.

Exchanging Currency:

Currency exchange is readily available in Egypt, and you'll find exchange offices (Forex bureaus), banks, and hotels offering currency exchange services.

Exchange rates can vary slightly between different sources, so it's a good practice to compare rates before exchanging currency. Banks often offer competitive rates.

It's advisable to exchange a small amount of your currency upon arrival at the airport or a bank to cover immediate expenses like transportation.

ATMs:

ATMs are widely available in cities, towns, and tourist areas throughout Egypt. They are a convenient way to access Egyptian Pounds.

Major credit and debit cards (Visa and MasterCard) are generally accepted at ATMs. However, it's a good idea to inform your bank about your travel plans to prevent any issues with your card.

Be aware of potential ATM fees imposed by your bank for international withdrawals. Also, consider using ATMs located in well-lit and secure areas.

Credit Cards:

Credit cards, particularly Visa and MasterCard, are accepted at many hotels, restaurants, and shops in tourist areas. American Express is less commonly accepted.

While credit cards are convenient, it's advisable to carry some cash for smaller establishments and in more remote areas where card payments may not be feasible.

Always check your card statement for any unexpected charges, and keep your receipts as proof of purchase.

Tipping:

Safety precautions

Egypt is a remarkable destination with captivating attractions. While it offers a unique and rewarding travel experience, like any other country, it's essential to be aware of safety precautions to ensure a secure and enjoyable visit. Here are some safety tips for travelers to Egypt:

Register with Your Embassy:

Register your travel plans with your embassy or consulate. This allows them to provide assistance in case of emergencies, such as natural disasters or political unrest.

Health Precautions:

Consult your healthcare provider before your trip to Egypt. Ensure you receive recommended vaccinations and take any necessary medications.

Drink bottled water to avoid waterborne illnesses, and be cautious with street food to prevent stomach issues.

COVID-19 Precautions:

Stay updated on COVID-19 travel requirements and guidelines. This includes vaccination and testing requirements, mask mandates, and quarantine rules.

Adhere to local COVID-19 restrictions and follow safety protocols, including mask-wearing and social distancing.

Transportation Safety

Use reputable transportation options, such as registered taxis, Uber, or reputable tour operators, to ensure your safety during transfers and excursions.

Exercise caution when crossing the street, as traffic can be chaotic in some areas.

Avoid Risky Areas:

Stay away from areas with a history of political unrest, protests, or demonstrations. Avoid participating in political discussions or gatherings.

Secure Your Belongings:

Keep your belongings secure at all times. Use a money belt or concealed pouch to store valuables, and be cautious of pickpockets in crowded areas and tourist spots. Be cautious of scams and fraudulent schemes, such as overpriced souvenirs, unofficial tour guides, or fake police officers. Always verify the legitimacy of service providers.

When possible, travel in a group or with a reputable tour company. Group travel can provide added safety and security. Carry a list of emergency contacts, including local authorities, your embassy or consulate, and your travel insurance provider.

When exchanging currency, use reputable banks or exchange offices. Be cautious of unlicensed money changers, as counterfeit currency can be an issue in some areas.

By following these safety precautions, you can enhance your security while exploring the wonders of Egypt. While the country is generally safe for tourists, being informed and prepared is crucial for a memorable and trouble-free trip.

Chapter Three

Vital tips for your trip

Moving around Egypt (Transportation:

Taxi, Train, Feluccas)

Egypt, with its vast cultural treasures, beckons travelers to explore its wonders. Navigating this captivating country is an essential part of your journey. Here's a comprehensive guide to transportation options in Egypt:

1. Taxi:

Taxis in Cities: Taxis are a common mode of transportation in Egyptian cities like Cairo and

Alexandria. Look for official taxis with meters. Ensure the meter is turned on or negotiate a fare before starting your ride. Taxi fares are generally affordable, but it's wise to have small denominations of Egyptian Pounds (EGP) for payment.

Ride-Sharing Apps: Ride-sharing apps like Uber and Lyft operate in major cities, providing a convenient and transparent way to travel. They offer similar services to taxis but with the added convenience of cashless transactions and GPS tracking.

2. Trains: Egyptian Railways: Egypt has an extensive railway network connecting major cities and tourist destinations. Trains are a comfortable and economical way to travel longer distances. They offer different classes, including air-conditioned and sleeper cars. Booking tickets in advance, especially during peak tourist seasons, is recommended. Train schedules and ticket information can be found on the Egyptian National Railways website.

Cairo Metro: In Cairo, the Cairo Metro is a fast and efficient way to navigate the city. It's divided into three lines, and metro tickets are quite affordable. Trains run regularly throughout the day.

3. Buses:

Local Buses: Local buses are available in cities and towns, providing a cost-effective means of getting around. However, they can be crowded and challenging to navigate for non-Arabic speakers. It's helpful to have your destination written in Arabic to show the driver.

Inter-City Buses: For longer journeys between cities, consider inter-city buses. They are a budget-friendly option, and different bus companies offer varying levels of comfort and amenities. Check schedules and book tickets in advance, if possible.

Domestic Flights:

Air Travel: When traveling between major cities or to remote destinations like Aswan or Sharm El Sheikh, domestic flights are a time-saving option. EgyptAir, the national carrier, operates numerous domestic flights. Be sure to book flights well in advance, especially during peak travel seasons.

Feluccas and Boats:

Feluccas: These traditional wooden sailing boats are a charming way to experience the Nile River. Felucca rides are available in cities like Aswan and Luxor. While they are slower than motorized boats, they provide a unique and tranquil way to view the river's scenery. Negotiate the price and duration of your felucca ride before setting sail.

Nile Cruises: For a more luxurious and leisurely experience on the Nile, consider booking a Nile cruise. These cruises offer a combination of sightseeing, dining, and entertainment, making them a popular choice for tourists exploring Upper Egypt.

Rental Cars:

Car Rentals: Renting a car in Egypt is an option, but it's advisable for experienced drivers familiar with local traffic and road conditions. Roads can be congested in cities, and driving styles may differ from what you're used to. International driver's licenses are often required, so check the specific requirements before renting a car.

Camels, Donkeys, and Horse-Drawn Carriages:

In some remote areas and desert landscapes, you may come across alternative modes of transportation, such as camel or horse-drawn carriage rides. While these can offer a unique experience, negotiate prices beforehand, and ensure the well-being of the animals.

Accommodation: Hotels and Hostels

Egypt, a land of ancient wonders and modern delights, offers a diverse range of accommodation options for travelers, catering to various budgets and preferences. Whether you're exploring the bustling streets of Cairo, unwinding by the Red Sea, or embarking on a historical journey along the Nile, you'll find suitable lodging choices in this captivating country.

Hotels:

Luxury Hotels: Egypt boasts a selection of world-class luxury hotels that redefine opulence. Cairo's iconic Mena House Hotel, nestled in the shadow of the Pyramids, offers breathtaking views and sumptuous suites. In Luxor, the historic Winter Palace Hotel, frequented by royalty and celebrities, combines classic elegance with modern amenities. Along the Red Sea, destinations like Sharm El Sheikh and Hurghada feature renowned chains like Four

Seasons and Ritz-Carlton, where guests can enjoy lavish accommodations, private beaches, and top-notch service.

Mid-Range Hotels: For those seeking comfort without breaking the bank, mid-range hotels are abundant. Cairo, Luxor, and Aswan have an array of options offering well-appointed rooms, reliable service, and often, swimming pools to beat the Egyptian heat. The mid-range hotels provide a balance between affordability and quality.

Boutique Hotels: Egypt's historic charm is well-reflected in its boutique hotels. In cities like Alexandria and Dahab, you'll find intimate and unique accommodations that often incorporate local aesthetics and offer a personalized experience. These boutique hotels are perfect for travelers who value character and authenticity.

Hostels:

Budget-Friendly Hostels: Egypt welcomes backpackers and budget-conscious travelers with a plethora of hostels. Cairo's downtown area, particularly around Tahrir Square, offers affordable dormitory-style accommodations.

These hostels are excellent for meeting fellow travelers and exploring the city on a shoestring budget.

Hostels by the Red Sea: Egypt's coastal destinations like Dahab, Sharm El Sheikh, and Hurghada have a thriving hostel scene. They often feature private rooms alongside dormitories and offer easy access to the region's stunning beaches and underwater treasures for divers.

Nubian Village Stays: For a truly unique experience, consider staying in a Nubian village along the banks of the Nile. These community-based accommodations provide a glimpse into the local way of life, with colorful houses, warm hospitality, and traditional meals.

When booking accommodation in Egypt, it's advisable to consider your itinerary, budget, and preferences. Reservations are often a wise choice, especially during peak tourist seasons. Regardless of where you choose to stay, Egypt's warm hospitality and rich culture will make your visit an unforgettable adventure

Language: Arabic Phrases for Travelers

When visiting Egypt, a basic understanding of Arabic phrases can significantly enhance your travel experience and help you connect with the locals. While many Egyptians working in the tourism industry speak English, making an effort to speak some Arabic phrases can be greatly appreciated and make your interactions more enjoyable.

Here are some essential Arabic phrases for travelers in Egypt:

Greetings:

Hello - مرحباً (Marhaban)

Good morning - صباح الخير (Sabah al-khayr)

Good evening - مساء الخير (Masa' al-khayr)

Goodbye - وداعًا (Wada'an)

Common Courtesies:

Please - من فضلك (Min fadlik)

Thank you - شكرًا (Shukran)

You're welcome - على الرحب والسعة (Ala al-rahb was-sa'ah)

Excuse me / Sorry - عذرًا (Aathran)

Basic Questions:

Yes - نعم (Naam)

No - لا (La)

What is your name? - ما اسمك؟ (Ma ismak?)

How much is this? - بكم هذا؟ (Bikram hatha?)

Where is...? - أين...؟ (Ayna...?)

How are you? - كيف حالك؟ (Kayfa haluk?)

Directions:

Left - يسار (Yasar)

Right - يمين (Yameen)

Straight ahead - مباشرةً (Mubashira)

Here - هنا (Huna)

There - هناك (Hunak)

Eating Out:

Menu - القائمة (Al-qa'ima)

Water - ماء (Ma')

I would like... - أريد... (Aureed...)

The check, please - الحساب، من فضلك (Al-hisab, min fadlik)

Numbers:

1 - واحد (Wahid)

2 - اثنان (Ithnan)

3 - ثلاثة (Thalatha)

10 - عشرة (Ashara)

Remember, Egyptians are generally appreciative of travelers making an effort to speak their language, even if it's just a few words. While you can get by with English in most tourist areas, learning a few Arabic phrases can open doors to deeper cultural experiences and warm interactions during your stay in Egypt.

Egypt Cultural Value

When visiting Egypt, a country steeped in history and tradition, it's essential to be mindful of its rich cultural values and norms. Respecting these values not only enhances your travel experience but also fosters positive interactions with the locals. Here's a guide to Egypt's cultural values for travelers:

Respect for Religion: Egypt is predominantly Muslim, and Islam plays a significant role in daily life. When visiting religious sites like mosques or during Islamic festivals, dress modestly, covering your shoulders and knees. It's customary to remove your shoes before entering a mosque and to be respectful and quiet.

Greetings: Egyptians value warm and polite greetings. Use common Arabic greetings like "Salam alaykum" (peace be upon you), which is often met with "Wa alaykum salam" (and upon you be peace).

Family and Hospitality: Family is central to Egyptian culture, and hospitality is a cornerstone. If invited to an Egyptian's home, it's customary to bring a small gift as a token of appreciation. Removing your shoes before entering is a sign of respect.

Dining Etiquette: When dining, wait for the host or elder to start the meal. Use your right hand for eating, as the left is traditionally considered unclean. If offered food or drink, it's polite to accept, even if it's just a small amount.

Punctuality: Egyptians tend to have a more relaxed view of time. While it's essential to be punctual for tours or scheduled activities, keep in mind that social meetings may have some flexibility.

Egyptians are known for their warmth and hospitality, and by being culturally sensitive, you can forge meaningful connections and leave with lasting memories of this incredible country.

Ethics of Life

As you journey through the enchanting land of Egypt, it's not only important to appreciate its awe-inspiring history and vibrant culture but also to understand and respect the country's ethics of life. These ethical values are deeply ingrained in Egyptian society and play a significant role in daily interactions. Here's a guide to Egypt's ethics of life for travelers:

Respect for Elders: Egyptians hold great reverence for their elders. It's customary to greet older individuals first and show deference in conversations. If offered a seat, especially on public transportation, consider offering it to an older person.

Kindness and Politeness: Egyptians are known for their warm hospitality and politeness. Simple gestures like saying "please" and "thank you" can go a long way in fostering positive interactions.

Friendship and Social Bonds: Building strong social bonds and friendships is highly valued. Egyptians are often eager to engage in conversations with travelers and share stories and experiences. Take the time to connect with locals to gain a deeper understanding of their way of life.

Tolerance and Diversity: Egypt is home to a diverse population, and tolerance for different cultures and religions is a core value. It's essential to show respect for all religious beliefs and customs, even if they differ from your own.

Generosity: Egyptians are incredibly generous and hospitable. If invited into someone's home, it's common for hosts to offer food and refreshments. Accepting these offerings with gratitude is a sign of respect.

Conservatism and Modesty: Egypt is a conservative country, particularly in rural areas and outside of tourist destinations. Dress modestly, covering shoulders, cleavage, and knees, to show respect for local customs.

Patience: Egyptian life often operates at a different pace than Western cultures. Be patient in everyday interactions, whether it's waiting in lines or dealing with bureaucracy.

Environmental Respect: Egypt is blessed with natural beauty, including the Nile River and its surrounding ecosystems. It's essential to respect the environment by disposing of trash responsibly and avoiding activities that could harm delicate ecosystems.

By embracing these ethics of life, travelers can not only navigate Egypt more harmoniously but also forge meaningful connections with the local people. Egyptians are known for their warmth and openness, and by showing respect for their values and customs, you'll undoubtedly have a richer and more rewarding travel experience in this remarkable country.

Egypt's local dishes

Egyptian cuisine is influenced by centuries of history and the region's diverse geography. Exploring the local dishes is an essential part of any trip to Egypt, and here are some must-try dishes and where to find them:

1. Koshari: This quintessential Egyptian dish is a hearty mix of rice, macaroni, lentils, chickpeas, and crispy fried onions, topped with a tangy tomato sauce and garlic vinegar dressing. It's a budget-friendly, vegetarian delight. For the best Koshari, head to the legendary Abu Tarek in

Cairo, a no-frills spot that's been serving this dish for decades.

2. Ful Medames: A beloved breakfast staple, Ful Medames consists of slow-cooked fava beans seasoned with olive oil, garlic, and spices, often served with boiled eggs, vegetables, and flatbread. You can find Ful Medames in street food stalls and local eateries across Egypt.

3. Shawarma: Although not originally Egyptian, shawarma has become a beloved street food. Thin slices of marinated meat, often lamb or chicken, are roasted on a vertical rotisserie and

served in pita bread with tahini, vegetables, and pickles. Try the best shawarma joints in Cairo's bustling street corners.

4. Molokhia: A nutritious green soup made from the leaves of the jute plant, molokhia is typically served with rice or bread and a choice of meat, like rabbit or chicken. It's a staple in Egyptian households and can be found in traditional restaurants throughout the country.

5. Ta'ameya (Egyptian falafel): Made from crushed fava beans or chickpeas mixed with herbs and spices, Ta'ameya is deep-fried to

crispy perfection. It's often served in pita bread with salad and tahini sauce. Visit the famous Mohammed Ahmed in Cairo for a Ta'ameya experience like no other.

6. Fish from Alexandria: When you're in Alexandria, don't miss the chance to savor freshly caught seafood. Restaurants along the Corniche offer a variety of fish dishes, from grilled seafood platters to seafood stew, all while enjoying picturesque views of the Mediterranean.

7. Umm Ali: This dessert is Egypt's answer to bread pudding. Made with layers of puff pastry, milk, nuts, and raisins, it's baked to perfection and served warm. You can find Umm Ali in many local bakeries and dessert shops.

While these dishes are easily found in larger cities like Cairo and Alexandria, be sure to also indulge in the local specialties in smaller towns and villages for an authentic taste of Egypt.

Egypt's Local Drinks

Egypt offers a range of unique and refreshing local beverages that are both satisfying and culturally enriching. Here are some of the must-try local drinks when visiting Egypt:

Hibiscus Tea (Karkadeh): This vibrant red tea is made from dried hibiscus flowers and is popular all over Egypt. It's often served hot, sweetened with sugar, or chilled with a dash of lemon. Karkadeh is not only delicious but also known for its potential health benefits, including lowering blood pressure and aiding digestion.

Mint Tea (Shai B'naana): A ubiquitous drink in Egypt, mint tea is made by steeping fresh mint leaves in hot water and sweetening it with sugar.

It's a soothing and refreshing choice, especially in the scorching Egyptian heat.

Sugarcane Juice (Asab): Freshly squeezed sugarcane juice is a delightful way to cool down. Vendors with sugarcane juicers can be found in most markets and along the streets. It's often served with a squeeze of lime for added zing.

Sahlab: A comforting and creamy drink, Sahlab is typically enjoyed in the cooler months. It's made by mixing ground orchid root with milk or water and then flavored with ingredients like cinnamon and nuts. It's a delicious and satisfying winter treat.

: This yogurt-based drink is a popular choice for quenching thirst. It's a mix of yogurt, water, and a pinch of salt, creating a slightly salty and tangy flavor. Ayran is not only refreshing but also helps combat dehydration in the Egyptian heat.

Licorice Tea (Erk Sous): Made from licorice root, this tea has a naturally sweet taste and is often consumed to soothe sore throats and coughs. It's a unique and herbal option to explore.

Dom: (local fermented yogurt drink): Dom is a yogurt-based drink that's lightly fermented, giving it a tangy flavor. It's often enjoyed with a sprinkle of salt and is known for its probiotic properties, aiding digestion.

Sobia: A popular Ramadan beverage, Sobia is made from rice and coconut milk, sweetened with sugar and flavored with a hint of cinnamon and vanilla. It's both creamy and refreshing, making it a favored choice during the holy month.

Egypt's local drinks add another layer to your cultural experience. They provide a taste of Egyptian tradition and a respite from the country's warm climate.

Shopping in Egypt

Shopping in Egypt is a delightful and culturally rich experience that offers travelers a unique opportunity to bring home not just souvenirs, but also a piece of Egypt's rich history and traditions. From bustling bazaars to modern malls, Egypt has a diverse shopping scene that caters to a wide range of tastes and budgets.

One of the most iconic shopping destinations in Egypt is the Khan el-Khalili market in Cairo. This historic market, dating back to the 14th century, is a labyrinth of narrow lanes and bustling stalls where you can find everything from colorful spices and aromatic oils to exquisite jewelry and handcrafted textiles. Haggling is a common practice here, so don't be afraid to negotiate for the best price.

For those interested in traditional Egyptian crafts, the Tentmakers' Bazaar in Cairo is a must-visit. Here, you'll find intricately embroidered textiles and quilts, all handmade by skilled artisans. These vibrant pieces are not only beautiful but also a testament to Egypt's rich textile heritage.

If you're looking for high-end shopping, head to the modern malls and boutiques in cities like Cairo, Alexandria, and Sharm El Sheikh. You'll find a mix of international brands and designer boutiques, making it easy to indulge in some retail therapy.

Egypt is also famous for its exquisite jewelry, particularly gold and silver. The Gold Souq in Cairo is a dazzling place to explore, with shops showcasing a stunning array of jewelry pieces, from delicate earrings to intricate necklaces. Egyptian jewelry often features intricate designs inspired by ancient symbols and hieroglyphs.

Don't forget to pick up some Egyptian spices while you're there. The country is known for its aromatic spices like cumin, coriander, and saffron. These make for fantastic souvenirs or additions to your own culinary adventures back home.

Whether you're exploring historic markets, seeking out traditional crafts, or indulging in modern retail therapy, Egypt has something to offer every shopper. So, be prepared to haggle, explore, and bring home a piece of Egypt's unique charm.

*Cairo Market

Cairo, the bustling capital of Egypt, is home to some of the most vibrant and historic markets in the world. Navigating the Cairo market scene can be an exhilarating experience for travelers, offering a unique glimpse into Egyptian culture and a chance to acquire a wide array of souvenirs and local treasures.

1. Khan el-Khalili Market: The Khan el-Khalili Market is an iconic labyrinth of narrow alleyways in the heart of Old Cairo. Dating back to the 14th century, this historic market is a sensory overload with its colorful stalls, the aroma of spices, and the melodious calls of shopkeepers. Here, you can find an array of goods, including traditional textiles, exquisite jewelry, ornate lanterns, and a variety of spices. Don't forget to brush up on your haggling skills, as bargaining is a common practice to secure the best deals.

2. Tentmakers' Bazaar: Located near the Khan el-Khalili Market, the Tentmakers' Bazaar is a hidden gem. This market specializes in intricate and handcrafted textiles, including quilts and wall hangings adorned with stunning embroidery. The craftsmanship on display here is a testament to Egypt's rich textile heritage, and these pieces make for unique and culturally rich souvenirs.

3. Gold Souq: For those with an eye for jewelry, the Gold Souq is a glittering paradise. This market offers an impressive array of gold and silver jewelry, often featuring designs inspired

by ancient Egyptian symbols and hieroglyphs. Whether you're in search of elegant necklaces, bracelets, or intricate rings, you'll find exquisite pieces to suit your taste.

4. Spices and Sweets: No visit to Cairo is complete without exploring the aromatic world of Egyptian spices. At markets like Khan el-Khalili, you'll discover stalls brimming with colorful spices like cumin, coriander, and saffron, along with a variety of dried fruits and nuts. These culinary treasures make fantastic gifts or additions to your own kitchen.

5. Local Cuisine: While not a traditional market, exploring Cairo's street food scene is an essential part of the market experience. Sample local delights like koshari (a mix of rice, pasta, and lentils), falafel, and shawarma from street vendors for an authentic taste of Egyptian cuisine.

Navigating the Cairo markets can be a thrilling adventure filled with cultural immersion and the opportunity to collect unique souvenirs. Whether you're in search of traditional crafts, jewelry, spices, or local cuisine, Cairo's markets offer a sensory journey through Egypt's rich history and culture. Remember to haggle with a smile and immerse yourself in the bustling atmosphere for an unforgettable shopping experience.

* Khan Market

Khan el-Khalili is a renowned historic market located in the heart of Cairo, Egypt, and is often considered a must-visit destination for travelers seeking an authentic and immersive shopping experience. This bustling marketplace has a rich history dating back to the 14th century, and it continues to be a vibrant hub of activity today.

Historical Significance: Khan el-Khalili's history is deeply intertwined with that of Cairo itself. It was originally built as a caravanserai, a place where traveling merchants could rest and trade their goods during their journeys along the Silk Road. Over the centuries, it evolved into a bustling market, making it one of the oldest and most historically significant markets in Egypt.

Labyrinthine Layout: Khan el-Khalili's narrow, winding streets and labyrinthine layout create a captivating and almost magical atmosphere. The market is a sensory feast, with the aroma of spices, the vibrant colors of textiles, and the melodious calls of shopkeepers filling the air. Travelers can easily lose themselves in the maze of alleyways, discovering hidden treasures and local artisans along the way.

Shopping Paradise: The market offers a diverse range of products, making it a shopper's paradise. Visitors can find traditional Egyptian crafts, such as intricately embroidered textiles, hand-blown glassware, and exquisite jewelry adorned with semi-precious stones. Additionally, Khan el-Khalili is famous for its aromatic spices, including fragrant blends like hibiscus tea and exotic spices used in Egyptian cuisine.

Haggling Culture: Haggling is an integral part of the shopping experience in Khan el-Khalili. Vendors often set their prices higher initially, expecting customers to negotiate for a better deal. Engaging in friendly haggling is not only accepted but also expected, allowing travelers to secure unique items at reasonable prices.

Cultural Immersion: Beyond shopping, Khan el-Khalili offers travelers a chance to immerse themselves in Egyptian culture. The market is an ideal place to people-watch, sip traditional

Egyptian tea or coffee in a local café, and strike up conversations with friendly locals.

Khan Market is a must-visit destination for anyone seeking an authentic Egyptian experience.

*Luxor Market

Luxor, often referred to as the "world's greatest open-air museum" due to its rich historical treasures, also boasts a vibrant market that adds a dynamic layer to the city's cultural tapestry. The Luxor Market, located on the east bank of the Nile River, offers travelers a unique shopping experience amid a backdrop of ancient wonders.

1. Souvenirs and Handicrafts: The Luxor Market is a treasure trove of souvenirs and handicrafts, where travelers can find a wide array of Egyptian artifacts and mementos. Traditional crafts, such as alabaster statues, papyrus paintings, and intricately woven textiles, are among the popular items to explore. These artifacts often feature designs inspired by ancient Egyptian symbols and pharaohs.

2. Authentic Egyptian Jewelry: Luxor is renowned for its exquisite jewelry, particularly pieces made with precious and semi-precious stones. Visitors can peruse a dazzling selection of gold, silver, and gemstone jewelry, often handcrafted by skilled artisans. From beautifully crafted rings and necklaces to elegant earrings, these pieces make for cherished souvenirs or meaningful gifts.

3. Spices and Perfumes: The Luxor Market also showcases Egypt's rich culinary and aromatic traditions. Travelers can explore stalls filled with aromatic spices like saffron, cardamom, and

cinnamon, as well as a variety of fragrant oils and perfumes. These make for unique and sensory-rich keepsakes of your Egyptian journey.

4. Alabaster Products: Luxor is famous for its high-quality alabaster, a translucent and beautiful stone. The market offers a plethora of alabaster products, including vases, lamps, and intricate sculptures. Many of these items are hand-carved by local artisans, adding an authentic touch to your shopping experience.

5. Haggling and Bargaining: Similar to other Egyptian markets, haggling is a common practice at the Luxor Market. Bargaining with shopkeepers can be an enjoyable and interactive part of the shopping experience, allowing travelers to secure the best prices and engage with local vendors.

6. Local Flavors: Don't miss the opportunity to sample Egyptian street food while exploring the market. You can savor traditional dishes like koshari (a hearty mix of rice, pasta, lentils, and spices) and indulge in fresh juices and sweets from nearby vendors.

The Luxor Market, set against the backdrop of Luxor's ancient wonders, offers travelers a chance to immerse themselves in Egypt's rich history and culture while shopping for unique souvenirs and authentic crafts. Whether you're interested in historical artifacts, jewelry, spices, or simply soaking in the vibrant atmosphere, the Luxor Market is a must-visit destination for any traveler in Egypt

* Aswan Market

Aswan, a city nestled along the banks of the majestic Nile River, is not only famous for its breathtaking natural beauty but also for its vibrant and culturally rich market scene. The Aswan Market, also known as the Souk al-Asr, is a bustling marketplace that offers travelers a unique opportunity to immerse themselves in the local culture and shop for a wide array of distinctive products.

1. Nubian Crafts and Artifacts: Aswan is a gateway to Nubia, a region known for its unique culture and crafts. The Aswan Market is a prime destination to discover authentic Nubian handicrafts, such as intricately woven baskets, vibrant textiles, and hand-carved wooden items.

These crafts often feature bold geometric designs and vibrant colors, reflecting the Nubian heritage.

2. Exquisite Jewelry: Aswan's market is a treasure trove for jewelry enthusiasts. Visitors can find an extensive selection of jewelry made from locally sourced gemstones, including the prized Nubian gold. Be it rings, necklaces, or earrings, the market boasts a variety of designs, from traditional to contemporary, appealing to diverse tastes.

3. Spices and Perfumes: Just like other Egyptian markets, Aswan Market is a haven for spice lovers. Aromatic spices, herbs, and exotic blends are on display, allowing travelers to explore the diverse flavors of Egyptian cuisine. Additionally, the market is rich with perfumes, essential oils, and fragrant incense, providing a sensory journey through Egyptian scents.

4. Handwoven Rugs and Carpets: The market is also known for its handwoven rugs and carpets that showcase intricate patterns and vibrant colors. These rugs are not only functional but

also works of art that can add a touch of Egyptian craftsmanship to your home.

5. Local Cuisine: As you explore the market, be sure to sample local street food and delicacies. Savor dishes like grilled kebabs, falafel, and fresh juices from the various vendors. The flavors of authentic Egyptian cuisine are sure to delight your palate.

6. Interacting with Locals: One of the highlights of the Aswan Market is the opportunity to engage with friendly locals. Whether you're haggling for prices or simply striking up a

conversation, interacting with the people of Aswan can provide insights into their way of life and their rich cultural heritage.

The Aswan Market is not only a place to shop but also a cultural experience that allows travelers to connect with the traditions and craftsmanship of the region. Whether you're seeking Nubian crafts, exquisite jewelry, or a taste of local flavors, the Aswan Market is a captivating destination that adds a layer of authenticity to your Egyptian journey.

Chapter Four

Tourism in Egypt / places to Visit and Time to visit

Cairo: The Capital of Egypt

Cairo, the bustling metropolis that straddles the banks of the Nile River, is not only the capital of Egypt but also one of the most historically and culturally significant cities in the world. With a history spanning thousands of years and a blend of modernity and tradition, Cairo is a captivating destination that offers travelers a diverse array of experiences.

Cairo's history dates back to the time of the pharaohs, and it has been the capital of Egypt for over a thousand years. The city is home to an incredible wealth of historical sites, including the awe-inspiring pyramids of Giza, the Sphinx, and the ancient temples of Luxor and Karnak. Exploring these iconic landmarks provides a profound connection to Egypt's ancient past.

The capital is often called the "City of a Thousand Minarets" due to its many mosques and Islamic architectural wonders. The historic neighborhood of Islamic Cairo boasts narrow alleyways, stunning mosques like the Sultan

Hassan Mosque and the Al-Azhar Mosque, and the medieval Khan el-Khalili market. The city's rich Islamic heritage is a testament to its role as a center of learning and culture in the Islamic world.

Cairo is home to world-class museums, including the Egyptian Museum in Tahrir Square, which houses a vast collection of ancient artifacts, including the treasures of Tutankhamun. The city also boasts the Coptic Museum, dedicated to Egypt's Christian heritage, and the Museum of Islamic Art.

While Cairo is steeped in history, it's also a dynamic and modern city. The skyline is punctuated by contemporary skyscrapers, and neighborhoods like Zamalek and Garden City offer a more tranquil and upscale atmosphere. The Cairo Opera House hosts cultural events, including music, dance, and theater performances.

Cairo's markets, or souks, are a feast for the senses. The Khan el-Khalili market is a bustling hub where travelers can shop for souvenirs, spices, textiles, and jewelry while savoring the scents of aromatic spices and local cuisine.

Egyptian dishes like koshari, falafel, and shawarma are a must-try for food enthusiasts.

The Nile River is the lifeblood of Egypt, and Cairo's riverfront offers enchanting views and opportunities for cruises, boat rides, and leisurely walks along the Corniche. At sunset, the city's bridges and buildings come alive with shimmering lights, creating a picturesque scene.

It's worth noting that Cairo's streets can be chaotic and congested, with a unique driving style that might be overwhelming for some travelers. However, this chaotic energy is part of the city's charm and character.

One of the most remarkable aspects of Cairo is the warmth and hospitality of its people. Egyptians are known for their friendliness and willingness to engage with travelers, making visitors feel welcome and valued.

Cairo is a city of contrasts, where ancient history coexists with modernity, and where vibrant markets blend with serene mosques. It's a city that can transport you back in time while allowing you to embrace the present. Cairo is not just the capital of Egypt; it's a cultural, historical, and sensory journey that leaves a lasting impression on every traveler fortunate enough to explore its streets and landmarks.

Alexandria

Alexandria, the Mediterranean jewel of Egypt, is a city steeped in history, culture, and natural beauty. Founded by Alexander the Great in 331 BC, Alexandria has been a center of learning, trade, and cosmopolitanism for centuries. Here are some highlights of this enchanting Egyptian city:

Alexandria's history is both illustrious and diverse. It was once home to one of the Seven Wonders of the Ancient World, the Pharos Lighthouse, and the Great Library of Alexandria, a renowned center of learning in antiquity. While these ancient wonders are no longer standing, their legacy lives on.

The city's picturesque location along the Mediterranean Sea provides stunning coastal views and a pleasant Mediterranean climate. The city's long, sandy beaches, such as Montaza Beach, offer a perfect escape from the hustle and bustle of urban life.

Alexandria is a blend of old-world charm and modern cosmopolitanism. The city's vibrant streets are lined with cafes, restaurants, and shops, offering a diverse range of international and local cuisine, making it a food lover's paradise.

The Bibliotheca Alexandrina, a modern reinterpretation of the ancient library, is a symbol of Alexandria's commitment to learning and culture. It houses millions of books, art galleries, a planetarium, and hosts various cultural events and exhibitions.

The city is dotted with historical landmarks, including the Qaitbay Citadel, a 15th-century fortress built on the site of the ancient Pharos Lighthouse. The Catacombs of Kom El Shoqafa, a remarkable underground burial site, showcases a fusion of Egyptian, Greek, and Roman styles.

Alexandria's diverse population and rich history have created a unique and cosmopolitan atmosphere. The city's residents are known for their friendliness, and visitors will find it easy to engage with locals, making their stay more enjoyable.

The city's maritime culture is evident in its bustling harbors and marinas. Travelers can enjoy boat rides along the coast, explore underwater archaeological sites, and even visit **the Naval Museum.** Alexandria has played a significant role in the literary world, being the hometown of the famous Greek poet Cavafy and the setting for works by renowned authors like Lawrence Durrell in "The Alexandria Quartet."

Alexandria's unique blend of history, culture, and coastal beauty make it a captivating and a good destination for travelers.

Siwa Oasis

Siwa Oasis, a hidden gem in Egypt's Western Desert, is a sanctuary of tranquility and natural beauty. Nestled near the border with Libya, Siwa Oasis is a remote and enchanting destination that captivates travelers with its unique charm.

Siwa is a lush haven in the midst of arid desert landscapes. Surrounded by date palm groves, olive orchards, and freshwater springs, it offers a stark contrast to the sandy dunes of the Sahara. It is inhabited by the Berber-speaking Siwans, who have maintained their distinct culture and traditions for centuries. Visitors can immerse themselves in the local way of life, from savoring traditional Siwan cuisine to witnessing ancient customs and rituals.

Siwa boasts historical sites like the Temple of the Oracle, where Alexander the Great sought divine guidance, and the Shali Fortress, a mud-brick citadel that stands as a testament to the region's history.

The oasis is known for its therapeutic hot springs, such as Cleopatra's Bath, where visitors can relax and rejuvenate in the mineral-rich waters.

Siwa's remote location offers exceptional stargazing opportunities. The clear desert skies are ideal for observing constellations and celestial wonders. It attracts adventurers with activities like dune bashing, sandboarding, and desert treks. The dramatic landscapes provide a dramatic backdrop for outdoor enthusiasts.

Above all, Siwa Oasis is a place of peace and serenity, making it an ideal destination for those seeking respite from the hustle and bustle of city life.

Siwa Oasis, with its pristine nature, offers a truly unique travel experience that allows visitors to connect with the rhythms of the desert and the timeless traditions of its people. It's a place where the past and the present coexist harmoniously, making it a destination like no other in Egypt.

Aswan

Aswan, a serene and culturally rich city in southern Egypt, is a hidden gem along the banks of the Nile River. Renowned for its breathtaking natural beauty, historical significance, and vibrant culture, Aswan is a must-visit destination for travelers seeking an authentic Egyptian experience.

Aswan's most striking feature is its stunning natural surroundings. The city is flanked by the Nile River on one side and the Nubian Desert on the other. The landscape is dotted with serene islands and granite outcrops, creating a picturesque backdrop for exploration. It has a long and storied history, with notable historical sites such as the Unfinished Obelisk, the Philae Temple, and the Nubian Museum. The Unfinished Obelisk is a colossal monument that offers insights into ancient Egyptian quarrying techniques, while the Philae Temple, dedicated to the goddess Isis, is a marvel of ancient architecture and carvings.

Aswan is the gateway to Nubia, a region with its own unique culture and traditions. Visitors can explore Nubian villages, engage with the warm and welcoming locals, and learn about their rich heritage. The Nubian Museum in Aswan provides a deeper understanding of Nubian history and culture.

Accessible by boat, Philae Island is home to the beautifully preserved Philae Temple complex. The island's tranquil setting and well-preserved ruins make it a captivating historical site that offers a peaceful retreat from the city. It is a popular starting point for Nile River cruises, allowing travelers to embark on journeys that showcase Egypt's iconic landmarks, including Luxor and the Valley of the Kings. Cruising along the Nile provides a unique perspective on Egypt's history and culture.

This island in the Nile boasts archaeological sites, including the ruins of ancient temples and fortifications. It offers a glimpse into Aswan's historical significance as a trading and strategic center in antiquity.

Aswan is renowned for its delicious Nubian cuisine. Local dishes such as ful medames (mashed fava beans), ta'meya (Egyptian falafel), and hawawshi (savory pastries) offer a flavorful taste of regional flavors. The Aswan High Dam, one of Egypt's engineering marvels, controls the Nile's annual flooding and provides electricity to the region. Visitors can tour the dam and learn about its impact on Egypt's development. Aswan offers an unforgettable Egyptian experience that reflects the country's diverse heritage and the timeless beauty of the Nile River.

Luxor

Luxor, often referred to as the "world's greatest open-air museum," is a captivating city in southern Egypt that beckons travelers with its rich history, archaeological wonders, and cultural treasures. Located along the banks of the Nile River, Luxor is a treasure trove of ancient Egyptian heritage and offers a mesmerizing glimpse into the country's past.

Luxor is steeped in history, and its most famous attractions are the ancient temples of Luxor and Karnak. These monumental temple complexes, dedicated to the god Amun-Ra, are adorned with colossal statues, obelisks, and intricate hieroglyphics. Walking through these ancient structures feels like stepping back in time to the era of pharaohs and gods.

Luxor is also the gateway to the Valley of the Kings and the Valley of the Queens, where many pharaohs, including Tutankhamun, were laid to rest. Visitors can explore the elaborately decorated tombs and marvel at the preserved art and hieroglyphs that tell the stories of the afterlife.

Luxor Temple, located in the heart of the city, is a stunning architectural masterpiece. At night, when the temple is illuminated, it creates a magical and romantic atmosphere that is perfect for an evening stroll.

The Nile River plays a central role in Luxor's charm. Taking a relaxing felucca ride on the Nile is a wonderful way to soak in the serene beauty of the river while enjoying the warm Egyptian sun and a gentle breeze.

Luxor's bustling markets, or souks, offer a wide range of local crafts, jewelry, spices, textiles, and souvenirs. Haggling is a common practice, so visitors can enjoy the lively art of negotiation while shopping for unique treasures.

Luxor is also a place where you can immerse yourself in Egyptian culture. Attend traditional music and dance performances or visit local cafes to savor authentic Egyptian dishes like koshari and kebabs.

The Luxor Museum houses a remarkable collection of artifacts from the region, including statues, jewelry, and mummies. It provides additional context and insight into the rich history of Luxor.

For a breathtaking panoramic view of Luxor's archaeological wonders and the Nile River, consider taking a hot air balloon ride during sunrise.

Luxor, with its awe-inspiring historical sites, serene river views, and vibrant culture, is a destination that leaves a lasting impression on all who visit. It is a place where the ancient world comes alive, and travelers can connect with the mysteries and marvels of Egypt's past while enjoying the warm hospitality of its people

Fayoum

Fayoum, often referred to as the "Land of the Lake" due to its proximity to Lake Qarun, is a tranquil oasis in Egypt that offers travelers a unique blend of natural beauty, historical sites, and cultural experiences. Located southwest of Cairo, Fayoum is an off-the-beaten-path destination that invites exploration.

The focal point of Fayoum's allure is Lake Qarun, the largest saltwater lake in Egypt. The lake is surrounded by serene desert landscapes, date palm groves, and lush agricultural fields, creating a picturesque setting for outdoor activities and relaxation.

Just outside of Fayoum, Wadi El-Rayan is a natural wonder comprising two connected lakes, surrounded by rolling sand dunes. It's a protected area that offers opportunities for hiking, bird watching, and swimming in the cool, crystal-clear waters of the lakes. Fayoum is steeped in history, dating back to ancient times.

It was an important center for agriculture and trade in antiquity. Visitors can explore the ruins of ancient cities like Medinet Madi and Karanis, as well as the Roman-era Hawara Pyramid, which is believed to be the final resting place of the famous philosopher and mathematician, Hypatia.

Fayoum is home to the Valley of the Whales (Wadi Hitan), a UNESCO World Heritage Site known for its exceptional fossil finds. Visitors can see the remarkably well-preserved skeletons of ancient whales and other marine life that once inhabited this area when it was covered by a prehistoric sea. The town of Fayoum itself is a hub of cultural activity, with traditional markets and local crafts. It's an ideal place to experience everyday Egyptian life away from the tourist crowds.

Fayoum is known for its delicious cuisine, including dishes like feseekh (fermented fish), ful medames (mashed fava beans), and delicious sweets like qara' 'asali (honey cookies). Local restaurants and cafes offer a taste of authentic Egyptian flavors. Lake Qarun offers opportunities for water-based activities such as fishing, sailing, and boating. Birdwatchers will also delight in the diverse bird species that flock to the lake's shores. Also, Fayoum is known for its friendly and hospitable locals who are always eager to engage with travelers and share their culture and traditions.

Fayoum is a destination where time seems to slow down, allowing travelers to savor the beauty and heritage of Egypt in a serene and welcoming environment.

Edfu

Edfu, a small yet historically significant town located on the west bank of the Nile River, is home to one of the best-preserved ancient temples in Egypt, making it a must-visit destination for history enthusiasts and travelers interested in Egypt's rich cultural heritage.

Edfu's crowning jewel is the Temple of Horus, dedicated to the falcon-headed god Horus, one of Egypt's most revered deities. This well-preserved Ptolemaic temple is a masterpiece of ancient Egyptian architecture and artistry. Its towering pylon entrance, impressive columns, and intricately carved reliefs provide a remarkable glimpse into the religious practices of ancient Egypt.

Edfu Temple is unique because it was built during the Ptolemaic period (237 to 57 BCE) and continued to be expanded during the Roman era. As a result, the temple reflects the influences of both dynasties, offering valuable insights into the merging of Egyptian and Hellenistic-Roman cultures. The temple's walls are adorned with hieroglyphic inscriptions that depict ancient Egyptian myths and rituals. These inscriptions provide a rich source of knowledge about the religious beliefs and ceremonies of the time.

The temple's hypostyle hall is a magnificent space with towering columns decorated with intricate carvings and hieroglyphics. It's a captivating area to explore and appreciate the grandeur of ancient Egyptian architecture.

Edfu Temple is famous for hosting the annual Festival of Horus, a reenactment of ancient myths and rituals. This festival, once a significant event in ancient Egypt, is still celebrated today and offers travelers a chance to witness traditional Egyptian culture and festivities.

Beyond its historical significance, Edfu offers a peaceful and picturesque setting. The town is surrounded by lush agricultural fields and the fertile banks of the Nile River, creating a tranquil ambiance for travelers. Edfu's location makes it an ideal stop for travelers exploring other ancient sites in Egypt. It's conveniently situated between Luxor and Aswan, making it a worthwhile addition to a Nile River cruise or a road trip through Upper Egypt.

Edfu, with its Temple of Horus is a captivating destination that offers an immersive journey into the past and provides a deeper understanding of the country's religious and architectural legacy.

Nile and the City of the dead

The Nile River, often referred to as the lifeblood of Egypt, is a majestic and historically significant waterway that has shaped the culture, history, and livelihood of the Egyptian people for millennia. Along its banks, particularly in Cairo, lies a fascinating and unique site known as the City of the Dead.

The Nile, stretching over 4,000 miles, is the longest river in the world and has played a central role in Egypt's development. It has nurtured fertile lands along its banks, making agriculture possible in the otherwise arid desert landscape. This lifeline has been crucial for Egypt's economy, providing water for irrigation and transportation. The Nile was the cradle of one of the world's earliest and most enduring civilizations, ancient Egypt. Its annual flooding, known as the inundation, deposited nutrient-rich silt along the riverbanks, enabling the cultivation of crops like wheat and barley that sustained the population.

Today, the Nile continues to be an essential part of modern Egyptian life. The riverbanks are dotted with bustling cities and towns, and the waterway itself is a vital transportation route, with feluccas and cruise ships carrying travelers and cargo.

Within Cairo, the City of the Dead (Arabic: "Qarafa") is a historic and unconventional cemetery that stretches for miles along the Nile's eastern bank. It's a unique blend of the living and the deceased, with thousands of mausoleums and tombs used as homes by people seeking refuge or economic opportunity.

The City of the Dead is not just a burial ground; it's a thriving community where people live, work, and raise families among the graves. Many residents have converted mausoleums into homes and shops, creating a surreal but culturally rich environment. Some of Egypt's most important historical figures are buried in the City of the Dead, and it's a place where history comes to life. Among the tombs are those of prominent Islamic scholars, politicians, and leaders. The community within the City of the Dead engages in various economic activities, such as carpentry, metalwork, and commerce, serving both the residents and visitors.

The City of the Dead offers a unique perspective on Egyptian culture and the resilience of its people. While it may seem unconventional to outsiders, it reflects the resourcefulness and adaptability of Egyptians in the face of challenges

The Nile River has been the cradle of Egyptian civilization, shaping the nation's history and culture. Along its banks lies the extraordinary City of the Dead, a living testament to the enduring spirit and adaptability of the Egyptian people, making it a remarkable and thought-provoking destination for travelers interested in the intersection of history, life, and death.

Chapter Five

Customs in Egypt

Egyptian Religion: Mosques, Synagogues, Coptic Churches

Egypt has a diverse religion that reflects the country's long history and cultural heritage. The primary religions practiced in Egypt include Islam, Christianity, and Judaism, each with its own sacred places of worship: mosques, synagogues, and Coptic churches, respectively. Here's a closer look at these religious institutions and their significance in Egypt:

Mosques:

Mosques are the places of worship for Muslims, who make up the majority of Egypt's population. Egypt is home to thousands of mosques, ranging from historic architectural marvels to smaller neighborhood prayer spaces. Some of the most prominent mosques in Egypt include:

Al-Azhar Mosque: Located in Cairo, Al-Azhar is one of the oldest universities in the world and a leading center of Islamic learning. The mosque itself is an architectural masterpiece and a symbol of Egypt's Islamic heritage.

Mohamed Ali Mosque: Perched atop Cairo's Citadel, this mosque offers panoramic views of the city. Its Ottoman architecture and towering minarets make it a prominent landmark.

Amr Ibn al-As Mosque: This mosque in Cairo is one of the oldest in Egypt, dating back to the 7th century. It holds historical significance as the first mosque built in Africa.

Sultan Hassan Mosque: Known for its intricate Mamluk architecture, this mosque is a prime example of Islamic design and craftsmanship. It features stunning courtyards, domes, and minarets.

Al-Hakim Mosque: Located in the heart of Cairo's Islamic Quarter, this mosque is famous for its intricate stucco work and is dedicated to the sixth Fatimid Caliph.

Synagogues:

Although Egypt's Jewish population has significantly declined over the years, the country still maintains a few synagogues that serve as historical and cultural landmarks. Some of the notable synagogues include:

Ben Ezra Synagogue: Located in Old Cairo, this synagogue has a rich history and is believed to have been constructed on the site where baby Moses was found in the Nile. Its medieval architecture and serene ambiance make it a popular attraction.

Shaar Hashamayim Synagogue: Situated in Cairo, this synagogue is an architectural gem with its ornate interior and beautifully preserved Torah scrolls. It is a symbol of Egypt's Jewish heritage.

Coptic Churches:

Coptic Christianity has a long and profound history in Egypt, and Coptic churches are significant religious institutions. The word "Coptic" refers to Egypt's indigenous Christian community. Some notable Coptic churches include:

Saint Mark's Coptic Orthodox Cathedral: Located in Alexandria, this cathedral is dedicated to Saint Mark, the founder of the Coptic Church. It is a beautiful and historic religious site.

Hanging Church (Saint Virgin Mary's Coptic Orthodox Church): Situated in Old Cairo, this church is one of the oldest in Egypt and is known for its unique location above the gatehouse of the Roman fortress of Babylon.

Saint Anthony's Monastery: Located in the Eastern Desert, this ancient Coptic Christian monastery is dedicated to Saint Anthony, one of the earliest Christian monks. It is a place of pilgrimage and monastic life.

Saint Catherine's Monastery: Located at the foot of Mount Sinai in the Sinai Peninsula, this

UNESCO World Heritage Site is one of the world's oldest working Christian monasteries. It houses a remarkable collection of religious manuscripts and icons.

Egypt's religious diversity, encompassing Islam, Christianity, and Judaism, is a testament to the country's rich history and cultural tapestry. These sacred places of worship, whether mosques, synagogues, or Coptic churches, not only serve as centers of religious devotion but also stand as architectural and historical treasures that reflect the enduring faith and heritage of Egypt's people. Visitors to Egypt have the opportunity to explore and appreciate the profound religious and cultural significance of these institutions, enriching their understanding of the nation's complex identity.

Egyptian museum

The Egyptian Museum, located in Cairo, is one of the world's most iconic and historically significant museums, often referred to as the "home of the pharaohs." Established in 1902, this renowned institution houses an unparalleled collection of artifacts, treasures, and antiquities that span over 5,000 years of Egypt's history.

Here's a glimpse into the significance and wonders of the Egyptian Museum:

The Egyptian Museum holds a central place in the world of archaeology and Egyptology. Its collection is a testament to Egypt's rich cultural heritage and serves as a vital resource for scholars and enthusiasts alike. The museum's very existence is a nod to Egypt's commitment to preserving its history and sharing it with the world.

The museum is home to an astonishing array of artifacts, including the world-famous treasures of Tutankhamun. The tomb of Tutankhamun, discovered in 1922 by Howard Carter, yielded a treasure trove of gold, jewelry, and other precious items. The Egyptian Museum houses the most comprehensive collection of these treasures, including the stunning golden death mask that has become an icon of ancient Egypt.

Beyond Tutankhamun's treasures, the museum boasts an extensive and diverse collection of over 120,000 items. These artifacts include statues, sculptures, jewelry, mummies, papyrus scrolls, and everyday objects from various periods of Egyptian history, including the Old Kingdom, Middle Kingdom, and New Kingdom.

The museum is also home to a captivating display of royal mummies, offering visitors a chance to come face to face with the pharaohs of ancient Egypt. The mummies are preserved in a climate-controlled environment, providing a glimpse into the lives of these revered rulers.

The Egyptian Museum hosts various exhibitions and displays that showcase different aspects of Egypt's history and culture. These exhibitions provide visitors with a deeper understanding of the civilization's art, religion, daily life, and achievements.

The museum building itself is a historic architectural marvel, blending traditional Egyptian and neoclassical design elements. Its grand façade and imposing columns make it an impressive sight in the heart of Cairo.

Future Grandeur:

While the Egyptian Museum has been a cornerstone of Egypt's cultural heritage for over a century, a new, state-of-the-art Grand Egyptian Museum (GEM) is under construction near the Giza pyramids. The GEM will be one of the largest archaeological museums in the world, providing an even more immersive and educational experience for visitors and serving as a testament to Egypt's continued dedication to preserving its heritage.

The Egyptian Museum in Cairo is a treasure trove of ancient wonders that allows visitors to delve into the rich and captivating history of Egypt. Its extensive collection, including the treasures of Tutankhamun and royal mummies, offers a profound and immersive journey through the civilization that has captivated the world for millennia. Whether you're a history enthusiast, an archaeology buff, or a curious traveler, the Egyptian Museum is a must-visit destination that provides a unique window into the mysteries and marvels of ancient Egypt.

Arts and Crafts in Egypt

Arts and crafts in Egypt are a vibrant reflection of the country's rich history, diverse culture, and deep-rooted traditions. Egyptian artisans have been honing their craft for centuries, producing a wide range of artistic creations that showcase their creativity and expertise.

Egyptian Jewelry: Egypt has a long history of jewelry-making, with artisans crafting intricate pieces using materials like gold, silver, semi-precious stones, and enamel. Traditional Egyptian jewelry often features symbolic motifs such as the Ankh, the Eye of Horus, and scarabs. Today, these exquisite pieces can be found in various markets and shops, including the famous Khan el-Khalili market in Cairo.

Papyrus Art: Papyrus, an ancient writing material made from the pith of the papyrus plant, has been used in Egypt for millennia. Egyptian artisans skillfully create papyrus art by painting intricate scenes of daily life, historical events, and deities. These unique artworks are not only visually captivating but also serve as a window into Egypt's rich past.

Handwoven Carpets and Rugs: Egypt is known for its hand woven carpets and rugs, which are often characterized by intricate patterns and vibrant colors. Carpets from regions like Upper Egypt are highly sought after for their quality and craftsmanship. These carpets can be found in bazaars and carpet shops throughout the country.

Calligraphy: Arabic calligraphy is an ancient and revered art form in Egypt. It is used to decorate mosques, religious texts, and various forms of artwork. Calligraphers use a variety of styles to create stunning compositions that often feature verses from the Quran or other meaningful texts.

Pottery and Ceramics: Egyptian pottery and ceramics are renowned for their beauty and diversity. Craftsmen create exquisite vases, dishes, and decorative items, often adorned with colorful glazes and intricate designs. The pottery tradition in Egypt has deep historical roots and continues to thrive today.

Woodwork and Inlay: Woodwork and inlay are traditional Egyptian crafts that have been practiced for centuries. Skilled artisans create intricate designs by embedding pieces of colored wood or mother-of-pearl into wooden furniture and decorative items. This meticulous craftsmanship can be seen in items like intricately designed chairs, tables, and jewelry boxes.

Traditional Clothing: Egypt's traditional clothing, such as the galabeya and kaftan, reflects the country's culture and history. These garments are often adorned with elaborate embroidery and patterns. Many tourists opt to purchase these clothing items as unique souvenirs of their visit.

Glassware: Egyptian glassware is known for its delicate beauty and intricate patterns. Skilled glassblowers create a wide range of items, from colorful perfume bottles to ornate glass lamps. The glass industry in Egypt has a long history, dating back to ancient times.

Exploring Egypt's arts and crafts is a captivating way to connect with the country's rich cultural heritage. Whether you're admiring the intricate details of a handwoven carpet, marveling at the beauty of papyrus art, or wearing traditional Egyptian jewelry, you're sure to appreciate the artistry and craftsmanship that have been passed down through generations in this ancient land.

Dressing Culture in Egypt

Egyptian dressing culture is a reflection of the country's diverse history, climate, and cultural influences. Traditional Egyptian clothing is not only functional but also carries significant cultural and historical meaning.

1. Traditional Attire:

Galabeya: The galabeya is one of the most iconic pieces of traditional Egyptian clothing. It is a loose-fitting, ankle-length robe made from natural fabrics like cotton or linen. Galabeyas are commonly worn by both men and women and are well-suited to Egypt's hot and arid climate.

Kaftan: The kaftan is another traditional garment, typically worn by women. It is a long, flowing robe often adorned with intricate embroidery and colorful patterns. Kaftans are commonly worn on special occasions and celebrations.

Hijab: The hijab is a common sight among Egyptian women, especially in urban areas. It is a headscarf worn for modesty and is often paired with a galabeya or modern clothing.

Kufi: Men may wear a kufi, a rounded cap, as a part of their traditional attire.

Modern clothing, influenced by Western fashion trends, is prevalent in urban areas and among the younger generation. Egyptians wear a wide range of clothing, from jeans and t-shirts to suits and dresses.

On special occasions, such as weddings and religious festivals, Egyptians often opt for more elaborate and embellished clothing. Women may wear embroidered dresses, while men may choose tailored suits.

The hot and dry climate of Egypt plays a significant role in clothing choices. Loose-fitting and breathable fabrics are preferred to help combat the heat.

Modesty is a key aspect of Egyptian dressing culture, influenced by Islamic values. Many Egyptians, particularly women, choose clothing that adheres to Islamic principles of modesty, covering the body except for the face and hands.

Regional Variation: Egypt's diverse regions may have unique clothing styles influenced by local traditions and climate conditions. For example, in Upper Egypt, people may wear clothing that differs from those in the coastal regions.

Egyptian dressing culture reflects a blend of tradition and modernity, with individuals choosing attire that suits their personal preferences and lifestyle. While traditional clothing remains an integral part of Egyptian culture, especially in rural areas, urban centers exhibit greater diversity in clothing styles. Whether donning traditional garb or contemporary fashion, Egyptians take pride in their clothing as an expression of identity and culture.

Music and Dance

Music and dance hold a special place in Egyptian culture, serving as vibrant expressions of the country's rich history and traditions. Here's a glimpse into the music and dance scene in Egypt:

1. Traditional Music: Egypt has a diverse range of traditional music styles that have evolved over centuries. One of the most iconic is classical Arabic music, characterized by the haunting melodies of the oud (a lute-like instrument), the enchanting rhythms of the tabla (drum), and the poetic lyrics that often draw from classical Arabic poetry. Traditional Egyptian music can be heard at weddings, religious celebrations, and cultural events.

2. Contemporary Music: Modern Egyptian music blends traditional elements with contemporary genres like pop, hip-hop, and

electronic music. Renowned Egyptian artists have achieved international acclaim, bringing Egyptian music to a global audience.

3. Folk Music: Egypt's rural regions have a rich tradition of folk music, featuring regional instruments like the simsimiyya and the mizmar. These musical styles often accompany traditional dances and are integral to local celebrations and festivals.

4. Dance: Egypt is famous for its captivating dance forms, with belly dancing (raqs sharqi) being the most well-known. Dancers showcase

graceful movements and intricate hip and torso articulations. Folk dances, such as the Saidi and Nubian dances, offer colorful and energetic performances that reflect the diversity of Egyptian culture.

5. Whirling Dervishes: The Sufi tradition of whirling dervishes is a mesmerizing form of spiritual dance in Egypt. Dressed in white robes and tall hats, the dervishes engage in a trance-like dance that symbolizes a spiritual journey towards enlightenment.

6. Influence on Cinema: Egyptian music and dance have had a significant impact on the country's film industry. Iconic Egyptian movies often feature memorable musical and dance sequences, further embedding these art forms in the nation's cultural identity.

Music and dance in Egypt are not only forms of artistic expression but also integral components of daily life and celebrations. Whether enjoying the rhythms of traditional Arabic music, the enchanting melodies of contemporary artists, or the hypnotic movements of dancers, experiencing Egyptian music and dance is a vibrant and unforgettable part of the country's cultural tapestry.

Nightlife in Egypt

Egypt's nightlife is wonderful, particularly in major cities like Cairo, Alexandria, and Sharm El Sheikh. Here's a glimpse into the nightlife in Egypt:

1. Cafes and Shisha Lounges: Egyptian nightlife often begins with a visit to a traditional café or shisha lounge. Locals and tourists alike gather to sip tea, coffee, or indulge in flavored shisha

(hookah), while enjoying lively conversations and sometimes live music.

2. Nightclubs: Egypt boasts a thriving nightclub scene, especially in urban centers like Cairo. These clubs feature a variety of music genres, from Egyptian and Arabic tunes to international hits. They often host renowned DJs and live bands, creating a dynamic atmosphere for dancing and socializing.

3. Bars and Pubs: Egypt offers a range of bars and pubs, from upscale venues with craft cocktails to cozy, traditional taverns. These

establishments are popular spots for enjoying local and imported beers, wines, and spirits.

4. Live Music Venues: For those seeking live music, Egypt offers numerous venues featuring local and international artists. Jazz clubs, blues bars, and concert halls showcase a variety of musical talents.

5. Nile River Cruises: In Cairo, nighttime Nile River cruises provide a unique way to enjoy the city's illuminated skyline. These dinner cruises often feature live entertainment, such as belly dancing and traditional music.

6. Themed Parties: Egypt hosts a range of themed parties and events, especially in tourist destinations like Sharm El Sheikh and Hurghada. These gatherings cater to various tastes, from beach parties to extravagant themed nights.

7. Shopping and Night Markets: Some markets and bazaars in Egypt come alive at night, offering a different shopping experience after sunset. These markets are perfect for those looking to buy souvenirs, textiles, and traditional crafts.

Egyptian nightlife is a dynamic blend of tradition and modernity, providing opportunities for both locals and visitors to unwind, socialize, and enjoy a diverse range of entertainment options. Whether you prefer dancing the night away in a club, sipping tea in a cozy café, or taking in the sights from a Nile River cruise, Egypt's nightlife has something for everyone.

Chapter Six

Activities to engage on in Egypt

Snorkeling

Snorkeling in Egypt is an extraordinary experience that allows travelers to explore some of the world's most renowned underwater wonders. With its crystal-clear waters, vibrant coral reefs, and abundant marine life, Egypt offers a paradise for snorkeling enthusiasts. Here's what you need to know for an unforgettable snorkeling adventure in Egypt:

Red Sea: The Red Sea, stretching along Egypt's eastern coastline, is a snorkeler's dream. Its warm waters are home to a breathtaking array of marine species and colorful coral formations. Popular snorkeling destinations along the Red Sea coast include Sharm El Sheikh, Hurghada, Marsa Alam, and Dahab.

Vibrant Coral Reefs: Egypt's Red Sea coast boasts some of the healthiest and most vibrant coral reefs in the world. The coral formations come in various shapes and sizes, providing shelter to an astounding variety of fish, sea turtles, and other marine creatures. The coral gardens offer a kaleidoscope of colors, making every snorkeling excursion a visual feast.

Marine Life: Snorkelers can encounter a diverse range of marine life in Egypt's waters. Keep an eye out for schools of colorful fish like butterflyfish, angelfish, and parrotfish. You may also spot larger species such as rays, reef sharks, and dolphins. Egypt's snorkeling sites offer something for both beginners and experienced snorkelers.

Accessibility: Egypt's snorkeling sites are easily accessible, whether you're staying at a beachfront resort or joining a guided snorkeling tour. Many snorkel spots are located just a short swim from the shore, making it convenient for travelers of all skill levels to explore the underwater world.

Snorkeling Tours: Joining a snorkeling tour is a popular option for travelers who want a guided experience. These tours often include transportation to prime snorkeling locations, equipment rental, and knowledgeable guides who can point out the best spots and marine life.

Ideal Climate: Egypt's Red Sea coast enjoys a warm and sunny climate throughout the year, making it a year-round destination for snorkeling. Water temperatures are comfortable, with visibility often exceeding 30 meters, allowing snorkelers to see the underwater world in all its glory.

Conservation Efforts: Egypt has taken steps to protect its coral reefs and marine ecosystems through the establishment of marine reserves and conservation programs. As a responsible traveler, you can contribute to these efforts by practicing eco-friendly snorkeling, such as avoiding touching or damaging the coral.

Night Snorkeling: For a unique and surreal experience, consider night snorkeling in Egypt. Many resorts and tour operators offer guided night snorkeling excursions where you can witness nocturnal marine life and bioluminescent creatures in action.

Snorkeling in Egypt offers an unforgettable opportunity to connect with the beauty of the underwater world. Whether you're a seasoned snorkeler or a beginner, the Red Sea's stunning coral reefs and abundant marine life promise an immersive and awe-inspiring adventure that will leave you with lasting memories of Egypt's aquatic treasures.

Camel Riding

Camel riding in Egypt is a timeless and quintessential experience that allows travelers to explore the country's iconic landscapes while immersing themselves in its rich cultural heritage. Riding a camel, often referred to as "the ship of the desert," offers a unique perspective and a memorable adventure.

Egypt's expansive desserts, including the Sahara and the Arabian Desert, provide a stunning backdrop for camel riding. Guided camel treks take you through these otherworldly landscapes, where towering sand dunes, vast plains, and rugged mountains create a mesmerizing panorama.

The most famous camel ride in Egypt is around the Giza Plateau, where you can embark on a camel journey that offers unparalleled views of the Great Pyramids, the Sphinx, and the ancient tombs and temples. It's a surreal and iconic way to experience Egypt's historical treasures.

Many camel riding experiences are led by knowledgeable Bedouin guides who share their deep understanding of the desert and its traditions. Travelers can gain insights into the Bedouin way of life, including their hospitality, music, and cuisine.

For a magical experience, consider a sunrise or sunset camel ride. The soft, golden light of dawn or dusk paints the desert in enchanting hues, creating a serene and tranquil atmosphere that's perfect for reflection and photography. Camels are well-suited to desert travel. Their surefootedness and ability to endure long journeys across the arid terrain have made them invaluable companions to Bedouin communities for centuries.

Camel rides in Egypt can vary in duration from short excursions to multi-day treks, allowing travelers to choose an experience that suits their preferences and available time.

Many camel riding tours offer the option to camp in the desert under a starlit sky, providing an authentic Bedouin camping experience. Enjoying a meal around a campfire and stargazing are unforgettable highlights. When engaging in camel riding, it's essential to choose operators that prioritize the welfare and treatment of their camels. Responsible tourism ensures that the animals are well-cared for and not overworked.

Camel riding in Egypt is not just a mode of transportation; it's a journey through time and culture. It allows travelers to connect with the country's ancient history, experience its natural beauty, and forge a connection with the Bedouin communities that call the desert home. Indeed, camel riding in Egypt promises an adventure of a lifetime.

Hiking

Hiking in Egypt offers adventurers a unique and often underestimated opportunity to explore the country's diverse landscapes, from desert treks to mountain trails. Here's a glimpse into the world of hiking in Egypt:

One of the most famous hiking destinations in Egypt is the Sinai Peninsula, home to Mount Sinai (Jebel Musa). Hiking to the summit of Mount Sinai, often undertaken at sunrise, is a spiritual and physically rewarding experience. The panoramic views from the top are breathtaking, and the journey is steeped in religious significance, as it is believed to be the place where Moses received the Ten Commandments.

Egypt's deserts, including the Sahara and Arabian Desert, offer a wide range of hiking opportunities. Adventurers can explore vast sand dunes, rugged canyons, and rock formations. The White Desert, in particular, is known for its otherworldly landscapes, featuring chalk rock formations that resemble surreal sculptures.

The Red Sea Mountains provide a striking backdrop for hiking enthusiasts. Trails lead through wadis (dry riverbeds) and past oases, offering glimpses of the region's unique flora and fauna. The Colored Canyon, near Dahab, is a popular destination known for its multicolored rock formations.

Egypt's oases, such as Siwa and Fayoum, provide a stark contrast to the surrounding desert. Hiking through these lush areas allows travelers to discover freshwater springs, palm groves, and ancient archaeological sites.

Infact, Egypt's historical and archaeological treasures often lie along hiking routes. The ancient city of Petra in Jordan, accessible via a multi-day hike from Egypt's Sinai Peninsula, is a prime example of a historic site accessible by foot.

Many hiking trips in Egypt include overnight camping under the starry desert sky. It's an opportunity to experience the tranquility of the desert and marvel at the brilliance of the night sky. It's essential to practice responsible hiking in Egypt by respecting local cultures and ecosystems, taking proper precautions for the desert environment, and leaving no trace behind.

Egypt's hiking opportunities are as varied as the landscapes themselves, promising unforgettable experiences for nature enthusiasts and history buffs alike.

Hot Air Ballooning

Hot air ballooning in Egypt is an exhilarating and unforgettable experience that offers travelers a unique perspective on the country's iconic landmarks and breathtaking landscapes. Here's what you need to know about hot air ballooning in Egypt:

The Hot Air Ballooning Capital: Luxor, often referred to as the "world's greatest open-air museum," is the premier destination for hot air ballooning in Egypt. The city's breathtaking historical sites, including the Valley of the Kings, Valley of the Queens, Karnak Temple, and Luxor Temple, are even more awe-inspiring from the sky.

Hot air balloon rides typically take place at sunrise when the weather is calm, and the lighting is perfect for photography. As you ascend into the sky, you'll witness the sun's first rays casting a golden glow on the ancient monuments and the lush banks of the Nile River.

One of the highlights of a Luxor hot air balloon ride is drifting over the Valley of the Kings. From this vantage point, you can see the intricate entrances to the tombs of pharaohs and nobles, carved into the desert cliffs, and gain a profound appreciation for the scale of these archaeological treasures. The nearby Valley of the Queens also reveals its secrets from the air. You'll have the opportunity to spot the tombs of queens, princesses, and high-ranking officials, each with its own unique hieroglyphic inscriptions and artwork.

As you float above the Nile River, you'll witness the serene beauty of its fertile banks, where lush green fields contrast with the surrounding desert. The river has been the lifeblood of Egypt for millennia, and seeing it from a hot air balloon is a serene and enchanting experience.

Hot air balloon operators in Luxor are experienced and prioritize safety. They conduct thorough safety briefings and ensure that all passengers are securely harnessed in the balloon's basket. Depending on your preference, you can choose to join a group flight with other adventurers or opt for a private hot air balloon ride for a more intimate experience.

Hot air ballooning in Egypt offers a once-in-a-lifetime opportunity to soar above some of the world's most remarkable historical and natural wonders. The sense of wonder and serenity experienced during a balloon ride over Luxor's ancient sites is unparalleled, making it a must-do activity for those seeking an extraordinary adventure in Egypt.

Chapter Seven

Egyptian Wonders

Egyptian mummies

Egyptian mummies are among the most iconic and mysterious artifacts in the world, offering a captivating glimpse into ancient Egyptian culture, beliefs, and burial practices.

Egyptian mummies are the preserved bodies of individuals from ancient Egypt, dating back as far as 3000 BCE. The process of mummification was a sacred and elaborate ritual believed to ensure the deceased's successful journey to the afterlife. Ancient Egyptians believed in an afterlife where the soul would need its earthly body. Thus, mummification was performed to preserve the body for this purpose.

Mummies provide valuable insights into Egyptian society, religion, and medical practices.

Types of Mummies:

Human Mummies: The most well-known mummies are those of humans, including pharaohs, nobles, and common people.

Animal Mummies: Egyptians also mummified animals like cats, dogs, and birds, often as offerings to gods.

Crocodile Mummies: The crocodile god Sobek was revered in Egypt, leading to the mummification of crocodiles.

Cairo Museum: The Egyptian Museum in Cairo houses an extensive collection of mummies, including those of famous pharaohs like Ramses II and Tutankhamun.

Luxor Museum: This museum in Luxor displays a fascinating collection of mummies and artifacts from the Theban necropolis.

National Museum of Egyptian Civilization: Located in Fustat, this museum houses mummies and offers insights into Egyptian history and culture.

Other Sites: Mummies can also be found in regional museums and archaeological sites throughout Egypt.

The mummification process involved several steps, including the removal of organs, dehydration, and wrapping in linen bandages. The removed organs were preserved in canopic jars.

Pharaohs and nobles received elaborate mummification treatments, while commoners often underwent simpler procedures.

Notable Mummies:

Tutankhamun: King Tut's mummy is perhaps the most famous in the world. His tomb, filled with treasures, was discovered nearly intact in the Valley of the Kings.

Ramses II: Also known as Ramses the Great, his mummy is one of the most well-preserved and impressive in Egyptian history.

Hatshepsut: The female pharaoh's mummy was discovered in the Valley of the Kings, adding to her legacy as a remarkable ruler.

While exploring mummies is a fascinating aspect of Egypt's heritage, it's crucial to approach these artifacts with respect and ethical considerations.

Preservation efforts and responsible tourism aim to protect mummies for future generations while ensuring their cultural significance is respected.

Mummification practices were not exclusive to Egypt. Other ancient cultures, such as the Incas and the Chinchorro people in South America, also mummified their dead.

Some European churches house naturally mummified bodies of saints and religious figures.

So in your travel, plan your visit to museums and archaeological sites in advance, as some exhibits may have limited access or require special tickets.

Respect photography rules, which may prohibit or restrict photography near mummies.

Learn about the history and significance of mummies through guided tours, books, or audio guides for a richer experience.

Exploring Egyptian mummies is a journey into the heart of ancient Egypt's religious beliefs, customs, and reverence for the afterlife. These well-preserved relics continue to captivate travelers and historians alike, offering a tangible connection to a civilization that left an indelible mark on human history. When visiting mummies in Egypt, travelers have the opportunity to unravel the mysteries of the past and gain a profound appreciation for the cultural heritage of this remarkable civilization.

The Sphinx

The Sphinx is one of Egypt's most iconic and enigmatic symbols, a colossal limestone statue with the body of a lion and the head of a pharaoh that has captured the imagination of people around the world.

The Sphinx is believed to have been built during the Old Kingdom of Egypt, around 2500 BCE, during the reign of Pharaoh Khafre.

It is situated on the Giza Plateau, adjacent to the Pyramids of Giza, forming an integral part of the complex that served as a grand burial site for pharaohs. It stands approximately 66 feet (20 meters) tall and 240 feet (73 meters) long, making it one of the largest monolithic statues in the world.

Its distinctive features include the human head, traditionally believed to represent Pharaoh Khafre, and the body of a recumbent lion, symbolizing strength and power.

The Sphinx is thought to have served as a guardian and protector of the Pyramids of Giza, watching over the tombs of the pharaohs and ensuring their safe journey to the afterlife.

Its form reflects the ancient Egyptian belief in the divine nature of pharaohs, with the lion symbolizing the king's strength and the human head representing his intellect and leadership.

Over the centuries, the Sphinx has suffered erosion and damage due to natural factors like wind and humidity.
Ongoing restoration efforts aim to preserve and protect this ancient wonder, and archaeological excavations around the Sphinx continue to reveal more about its history and surroundings.

Despite centuries of study, the Sphinx remains shrouded in mystery. The original purpose of the statue and the identity of the pharaoh it represents are topics of ongoing debate and exploration.

Theories about hidden chambers or tunnels beneath the Sphinx continue to capture the imagination of archaeologists and explorers.

The Sphinx and the nearby Pyramids of Giza draw millions of tourists each year, making them some of the most visited archaeological sites in the world. Visitors can explore the Giza Plateau, admire the Sphinx up close, and learn about its history and significance through on-site displays and guided tours.

The Sphinx stands as a timeless symbol of ancient Egypt's grandeur and mystery, inviting travelers and historians to contemplate its significance and marvel at its enduring presence on the Giza Plateau. Whether seen against the backdrop of the pyramids or illuminated by the setting sun, the Sphinx remains a testament to the craftsmanship and cultural significance of ancient Egypt.

Karnak Temple

Karnak Temple, located in the ancient city of Thebes (modern-day Luxor), is one of Egypt's most spectacular and significant archaeological sites. This vast temple complex, dedicated primarily to the god Amun-Ra, offers a glimpse into the grandeur of ancient Egyptian architecture, religion, and history. Karnak Temple is a testament to the enduring devotion of numerous pharaohs over the centuries. Its construction began in the Middle Kingdom (around 2000 BCE) and continued for more than a thousand years, through the New Kingdom period and beyond.

The temple complex served as a center for religious worship, rituals, and administrative activities, making it one of the most important religious sites in ancient Egypt.

Karnak is a vast complex comprising multiple temples, chapels, pylons (massive gateways), obelisks, and columns. Its sheer size and architectural diversity are awe-inspiring.

The Great Hypostyle Hall, in particular, stands out with its forest of 134 massive columns, each adorned with intricate hieroglyphs and reliefs.

A long avenue of sphinxes, with ram-headed sphinxes on one side and human-headed sphinxes on the other, originally connected Karnak Temple to Luxor Temple, creating a ceremonial pathway used during religious festivals.

Within the complex, there is a large artificial lake known as the Sacred Lake. It was used for ceremonial and purification purposes and is believed to have been home to sacred crocodiles. Karnak was dedicated primarily to the god Amun-Ra, the king of the gods in ancient Egyptian mythology. The temple complex also honored other deities, including Mut and Khonsu.

It played a central role in the annual Opet Festival, where statues of Amun, his wife Mut, and their son Khonsu were carried in a grand procession between Karnak and Luxor temples.

Karnak Temple has undergone extensive restoration and preservation efforts over the years. The Egyptian government, along with international organizations, has worked tirelessly to protect and maintain this cultural treasure.

Today, Karnak Temple is open to visitors from around the world. Exploring the site offers a mesmerizing journey through ancient history, with opportunities to admire the colossal statues, hieroglyphic inscriptions, and intricate reliefs that adorn its structures.

Sound and Light shows held in the evenings provide a captivating way to experience the temple complex, as illuminated projections and narrations bring its history to life.

Karnak Temple, along with the entire city of Luxor, has been designated as a UNESCO World Heritage Site, recognizing its immense cultural and historical significance.

Karnak Temple stands as a testament to the architectural prowess, religious devotion, and cultural achievements of ancient Egypt. Its colossal columns, majestic pylons, and intricate reliefs continue to inspire awe and wonder, allowing modern-day visitors to connect with the grandeur of an ancient civilization that thrived along the banks of the Nile for millennia.

The pyramids of Giza

The Pyramids of Giza, located on the Giza Plateau just outside Cairo, Egypt, are one of the world's most iconic and enduring symbols of ancient civilization. These colossal structures, built during the Old Kingdom period of ancient Egypt, continue to captivate the imagination of people worldwide.

The Pyramids of Giza were constructed over 4,000 years ago, during the Fourth Dynasty of the Old Kingdom, around 2580-2560 BCE.

They served as grand tombs for pharaohs, including Khufu (Cheops), Khafre, and Menkaure, and were intended to ensure a successful journey to the afterlife.

The three main pyramids at Giza are: the Great Pyramid of Khufu, the Pyramid of Khafre, and the Pyramid of Menkaure. The Great Pyramid is the largest and most famous.

The Great Pyramid originally stood at 146.6 meters (481 feet) but is slightly shorter today due to the loss of its outer casing stones.

The precision and engineering prowess exhibited in the construction of these pyramids are awe-inspiring. The massive stones were quarried and transported from various locations, and the pyramids were aligned with incredible precision.

The pyramids were designed as monumental tombs and were laden with religious and symbolic significance. The shape of the pyramid, with its pointed apex, was believed to facilitate the deceased pharaoh's ascent to the heavens.

Inside the pyramids, intricate passageways lead to burial chambers, where the pharaohs' bodies, treasures, and items for the afterlife were placed.

The construction methods used in building the pyramids continue to be a subject of fascination and debate. Various theories abound, including ideas about the use of ramps, lever systems, and the organization of a vast labor force.

The precise mathematical and astronomical knowledge required for the alignment of the pyramids has led some to speculate about their connection to extraterrestrial or advanced ancient civilizations.

The Pyramids of Giza are top tourist destinations in Egypt. Visitors can explore the Giza Plateau and enter the inner chambers of some pyramids. The Giza complex also features an informative visitor center and the Solar Boat Museum, where an ancient ceremonial boat that once belonged to Pharaoh Khufu is displayed.

Preservation efforts are ongoing to protect the pyramids from environmental factors and wear and tear caused by tourism.

Measures such as limiting access to certain areas and employing non-invasive restoration techniques aim to ensure the pyramids' longevity.

The Pyramids of Giza are not only remarkable for their historical and architectural significance but also for the sense of wonder and awe they inspire in all who visit. They stand as a testament to the ingenuity, engineering prowess, and cultural achievements of ancient Egypt, as well as the enduring allure of the mysteries that surround them. Exploring the Giza Plateau and standing before these colossal monuments is an experience that allows travelers to connect with the timeless legacy of one of the world's greatest civilizations.

Final Tips for your stay and visit in Egypt

Before leaving Egypt

As you prepare to conclude your visit to Egypt, here are some final tips and considerations to ensure a memorable and smooth departure:

1. Currency Exchange: Prior to departing Egypt, make sure to exchange any remaining Egyptian

pounds (EGP) for your home currency at authorized currency exchange offices or banks. It's essential to retain small denominations for tips and small purchases at the airport or during your departure.

2. Souvenirs and Gifts: If you plan to purchase souvenirs or gifts, do so in advance of your departure. Souvenir shops and markets are readily available throughout Egypt, but it's a good idea to complete your shopping a day or two before leaving to avoid any last-minute rush.

3. Packing and Luggage: Double-check your luggage to ensure that you haven't forgotten anything important. Keep essential documents, such as your passport, tickets, and travel insurance, within easy reach in your carry-on bag. Ensure that your checked luggage complies with your airline's baggage weight limits.

4. Airport Procedures: Arrive at the airport well in advance of your departure time, as airports in Egypt can be busy, especially during peak travel periods. Be prepared to go through security checks and customs before boarding your flight.

5. Local Sim Card Return: If you purchased a local SIM card during your stay, be sure to remove it from your phone and return it to the vendor or dispose of it properly. You may also inquire about recycling options for electronic waste if needed.

6. Gratuities and Tipping: Tipping, or "baksheesh," is customary in Egypt for various services, from hotel staff to tour guides and drivers. Ensure you have enough cash on hand for tipping, especially during your departure when you may receive assistance with luggage or other services.

7. Departure Tax: Some international departure taxes may be included in your flight ticket, but it's a good idea to check with your airline or travel agent to confirm if any additional fees apply.

8. Check Flight Details: Confirm your flight details, gate number, and boarding time on the day of departure. Flight schedules can occasionally change, so it's a good practice to stay informed.

Final Sightseeing: If you have a few hours before your flight, consider visiting a nearby attraction or enjoying a last meal at a local restaurant. Make the most of your remaining time in Egypt.

Safety Precautions: As with any international travel, remain vigilant and keep an eye on your belongings, especially at crowded places like airports and tourist hubs.

These tips will help you to cherish and have a memorable visit and wish to visit again.

Egyptian souvenirs to take home

Goodbye from Egypt

As you bid farewell to Egypt, consider taking home some delightful souvenirs to preserve the memories of your visit to this captivating country. Egypt offers a wealth of unique and culturally significant items that make for wonderful keepsakes and gifts:

Papyrus Art: Egyptian papyrus is famous for its use in ancient manuscripts. You can purchase beautifully hand-painted papyrus art depicting scenes from ancient Egypt, hieroglyphics, or intricate designs.

Spices and Herbs: Explore the vibrant world of Egyptian cuisine by bringing home an assortment of aromatic spices like cumin, coriander, and saffron. These can enhance your cooking and remind you of the flavors of Egypt.

Perfumes and Oils: Egypt is known for its fragrances, and you can find an array of perfumes and essential oils infused with scents like jasmine, lotus, and sandalwood. These make for excellent gifts or personal indulgences.

Jewelry: Traditional Egyptian jewelry often features symbols like the ankh, scarab beetle, and Eye of Horus. Consider buying a piece of silver or gold jewelry as a keepsake or gift for loved ones.

Alabaster Crafts: Luxor is renowned for its alabaster workshops. You can find exquisite alabaster vases, statues, and decorative items that showcase the craftsmanship of local artisans.

Traditional Clothing: Traditional Egyptian clothing like galabeyas (loose-fitting robes) and shawls can be unique and comfortable souvenirs. They are often adorned with colorful patterns and embroidery.

Copper and Brass Items: From intricately designed lanterns to tea sets and trays, Egyptian copper and brass items are not only beautiful but also representative of the country's artisanal heritage.

Cartouches: These are personalized hieroglyphic nameplates, and they make for an authentic and personalized keepsake from Egypt.

Handmade Carpets and Rugs: Egypt produces exquisite handmade carpets and rugs, often featuring intricate patterns and rich colors. They can be a bit heavy but make for a timeless addition to your home decor.

Traditional Musical Instruments: If you're a music enthusiast, consider buying an Egyptian musical instrument like a darbuka (goblet drum) or an oud (a lute-like instrument).

As you collect these souvenirs, remember to support local artisans and purchase from reputable stores to ensure the authenticity and quality of your purchases. These mementos will serve as lasting reminders of your incredible journey through Egypt, a land steeped in history, culture, and timeless beauty. Goodbye from Egypt, and may your memories of this remarkable country continue to inspire you.

Printed in Great Britain
by Amazon